China Briefing, 1985

中国

Also of Interest

†*China Briefing, 1984,* edited by Steven M. Goldstein

†*China Briefing, 1982,* edited by Richard C. Bush

†*China Briefing, 1981,* edited by Robert B. Oxnam and Richard C. Bush

†*China Briefing, 1980,* edited by Robert B. Oxnam and Richard C. Bush

China Geographer, No. 12: The Environment, edited by Clifton W. Pannell and Christopher L. Salter

†*Modernizing China: Post-Mao Reform and Development,* edited by A. Doak Barnett and Ralph N. Clough

†*The Making of Foreign Policy in China: Structure and Process,* A. Doak Barnett

†*The Government and Politics of the PRC: A Time of Transition,* Jürgen Domes

†*China Through the Ages,* Franz Michael, with an Introduction by Robert Scalapino

Power and Policy in the PRC, edited by Yu-ming Shaw

Mainland China: Politics, Economics, and Reform, edited by Yu-ming Shaw

Six Chapters of Life in a Cadre School: Memoirs from China's Cultural Revolution, Yang Chiang, translated and annotated by Djang Chu

†Available in hardcover and paperback.

China Briefing, 1985

edited by
John S. Major

Published in cooperation with the
China Council of The Asia Society

中国

Routledge
Taylor & Francis Group
LONDON AND NEW YORK

First published 1986 by Westview Press

Published 2018 by Routledge
52 Vanderbilt Avenue, New York, NY 10017
2 Park Square, Milton Park, Abingdon, Oxon OX14 4RN

Routledge is an imprint of the Taylor & Francis Group, an informa business

Library of Congress ISSN: 0740-8005

ISBN 13: 978-0-367-00651-8 (hbk)
ISBN 13: 978-0-367-15638-1 (pbk)

Contents

Preface

The China Council of The Asia Society is a non-profit, non-partisan educational organization. In keeping with its mission of providing accurate and impartial information on China and U.S.-China relations to the American public, it has in every year but one since 1980 published an annual *China Briefing*. It is a pleasure to present *China Briefing, 1985* to the large and growing number of persons in the United States and overseas who wish to deepen their understanding of contemporary China.

As with *China Briefing, 1984*, all of the essays in this volume were specially commissioned and have not been previously published. Although each volume of the *China Briefing* series is intended to stand on its own as a review of the year in question, it is also our hope that the volumes taken together will serve as a cumulative account of events in China over a period of years marked by rapid and exciting changes. Some topics—for example, politics and international relations—are dealt with in these volumes year after year; others, such as culture and education, appear less frequently. Thus the general approach of Merle Goldman's article on culture in *China Briefing, 1984* remains valid in the current year; Peter Seybolt's essay on education in this volume provides a review of salient events in the past few years as well as detailed information for 1985. This year, for the first time since 1982, a chapter is devoted exclusively to Taiwan.

I wish to express my appreciation to all of the authors for producing their chapters with both the necessary speed and efficiency and the hoped-for high quality. Harry Harding's incisive comments as manuscript reader made my editorial task a light one. Corey McDonnell, the China Council's program assistant, handled the manuscript preparation with her customary cheerfulness and efficiency, and in addition prepared the chronology that appears at the end of this volume. Our typists, Mike Franks and Lorri Kaye, were models of coolness and accuracy under pressure. Finally, Susan McEachern, acquisitions editor at Westview Press, was a delight to work with and has my deepest thanks for her patience and cooperation.

John S. Major

Source: U.S. Department of State, "Background Notes: China," December 1983.

1
Domestic Politics

David Bachman

If reform dominated the news in Chinese domestic politics in 1984,[1] the biggest story to emerge in Chinese politics in 1985 was the discovery of the limits of reform. This is not to say that reform is dead in China, but that throughout 1985, especially in the second half of the year, a diffuse but very broad segment of the Chinese polity made its opposition to elements of the reform program clear. Students, cadres, urban dwellers, national minorities, and others all expressed some degree of dissatisfaction with aspects of the reform program. The views of these groups, the unintended negative consequences of the reforms themselves, the pervasive corruption found in the Chinese Communist Party (CCP), and the failure of official ideology to guide and inspire the Party and the Chinese people, left Deng Xiaoping and his allies with the need to rethink their strategy and tactics fundamentally.

The reformers did advance the transformation of the Chinese economic system during 1985 and appear to have achieved a number of important goals that seemed to strengthen their political position. In the first half of 1985, major programmatic reforms of the science and technology and educational systems were launched. Prices for many agricultural products were allowed to reflect supply and demand. The rural reforms were further consolidated. A major shake-up of the military was undertaken. Personnel changes and policy decisions made at the National Party Conference in September further aided the reformers' cause. While there may have been opposition to these developments, it did not hinder the formulation and at least partial implementation of these measures.

However, in the second half of 1985, the Dengist revolution from above in the name of reform bumped up against "the social limits of politically induced change."[2] Groups, such as students and urban dwellers, which had previously gone along with the reforms now began to express anxiety or dissatisfaction with elements of the reformers' program. By itself, this opposition may not have been very threatening to Deng and his allies. But when coupled with the revelation of wide-spread corruption in the Party and the government, it presented China's top reformers with a basic and not easily resolved problem by the end of the year. In the short-run (and perhaps longer), some of the key elements of the reformers' constituency had serious doubts about the reform program. Moreover, by the end of the year, it was an open question whether the Party had become so corrupt that it was incapable of pushing through further initiatives. To rephrase the dilemma facing Deng, Hu Yaobang, Zhao Ziyang, and other reformers, they had to continue to rely on an organizational weapon that may no longer be a reliable instrument in carrying out the reforms in the face of mounting opposition from society. Whether the leadership can minimize social discontent while reinvigorating the Party and other major bureaucratic organizations is the crucial issue as China enters the Seventh Five Year Plan (1986–1990).

In this essay, we will examine the progress reformers made in advancing their revolution from above during the first half of 1985. Next, we will turn to ideological developments. Third, we will look at the transformation of the Party leadership, and particularly the emergence of a new elite from a series of meetings in September 1985. We will then focus on the problems and the sources of opposition facing Deng and his colleagues in the second half of 1985. Finally we will conclude with some brief comments on prospects for China in 1986 and beyond.

The Reform/Revolution from Above

In 1985, the Chinese leadership achieved successes in five major areas: science and technology, education, prices, the rural sector, and the military. In addition, continued progress was made in two other areas: the development of the legal system and the open door policy (at least until mid-1985). We shall briefly review the policies in each of these areas.

On March 13, 1985, the Central Committee of the Chinese Communist Party (CCP) released a major document on the reform of the science and technology management system. The goal of this reform was to integrate scientific and technological developments more thoroughly with economic construction. Science and technology were to concentrate on applied, as opposed to basic, research. Scientific research institutes were to engage in contract work for economic enterprises. A "technology market" was to be established. Science foundations, apparently modeled on the U.S. National Science Foundation, were to be founded. Management of research institutes was to be reformed and made more responsive to a changing domestic economy.[3] Many of the individual proposals in this document were not new developments in 1985. Some had been discussed since 1979. What was important was the comprehensive nature of the document, and the imprimatur of Central Committee approval.

Two months later, the Central Committee announced another major decision, this time on the reform of the educational system. In line with the science and technology decision, this document gave colleges and universities expanded autonomy in managing their own affairs, in contracting out their services to other institutions, and in enrolling students who paid their own tuition. The document also stipulated that a 9-year mandatory system of education be gradually implemented. A scholarship program for college students was to be introduced, and the previous system whereby all college students within the state plan had their fees paid by the state was to change.[4]

In early 1985, it was announced that prices for most agricultural commodities could fluctuate with market demands, or within broad price bands set by the state. Pork, vegetables, and other perishable products were subject to market regulation, though the prices for grain, oil, and other basic commodities remained fixed or these commodities remained subject to rationing. Prices for various industrial commodities, particularly when a surplus of the product existed, were increasingly subject to the dictates of the market. Even the determination of prices of previously controlled items, such as railway haulage fees and coal, was to be based increasingly upon economic factors.[5] China seemed to be making real progress in dealing with the classic stumbling block of all reform efforts in socialist economic systems: irrational prices.

The rural reforms were further consolidated in the Central Committee's Document No. 1. State procurement quotas for agricultural products were abolished. From now on, grain and cotton would be sold to the state on the basis of contracts. Other agricultural commodities would be supplied on the basis of market relations. The expansion of small towns and cities in the countryside was encouraged. All round development of the rural economy was promoted, especially rural industry.[6]

Finally, and perhaps most significant of all the reform efforts of the first half of 1985, the People's Liberation Army was also transformed. The army was to be reduced in size by a million troops over 1985–1986, with many of the retirees to come from the officer corps. The eleven military regions were to be reduced to seven, further diminishing the size of the officer corps. Younger, more professionally competent officers were promoted, and older officers who had grumbled about Deng's reforms were forced out of power.[7] While it is conventional wisdom that a number of veterans of the PLA oppose Deng's reforms, it is hard to argue that the military has fought the reformers relentlessly over recent policy changes. Nonetheless, this cut in the military and the continuing removal of the old guard no doubt strengthen Deng's political position. Moreover, U.S. military sales, of turbine engines to the Chinese navy, of artillery manufacturing facilities to the ground forces, and proposed sales of advanced avionics to the air force, may further encourage the military to support the Dengist line.[8]

In addition to these major initiatives, progress was made in other areas of concern to Chinese leaders. The drive towards legal codification continued with new inheritance and accountancy laws taking effect, and a law on state-owned enterprises was under consideration. In connection with the open door policy, a law on economic contracts with foreigners went into force, and detailed regulations on the patent law were formulated. More ports were opened to foreign trade, a new round of bidding for off-shore oil development was solicited, and the Chinese also declared that foreigners could participate in the development of on-shore oil fields.

Thus, through the first half of 1985, Deng Xiaoping and his allies seemed to have no trouble maintaining the political initiative. Major new reforms were launched, and existing reforms were consolidated and further developed. This is not to say that the reforms have worked, or been implemented as the policy documents say they should. Opposition elements did not object to the reforms, or if they did, their views went unheeded. The revolution from above in the name of reform seemed to be well on track throughout the first part of 1985. But developments in other areas suggested that the reformist groups' hold over the political situation was more tenuous than their successes in pushing these reforms through might imply. Serious economic problems were already apparent by March and April 1985, and developments in other areas were not overly auspicious.

Rethinking Ideology

While reforms were undertaken in the areas of science, education, the economy, and the military in early 1985, Deng Xiaoping and Hu Yaobang were rethinking their views on ideology. In December 1984, it appeared to many foreign observers that China was preparing to jettison Marxism. But throughout 1985, Deng and Hu made it clear that capitalism was unacceptable to the leadership and that reform was merely a means of perfecting socialism. To be sure, the type of socialism being built in China would be a pragmatic type heretofore unseen in socialist systems. But for Deng et al., the four basic principles—Party leadership, the socialist road, Marxist-Leninist-Mao Zedong thought, and the people's democratic dictatorship—remained inviolable. Some might argue that

Deng's position on a number of ideological issues is a retreat, either to combat his opponents or forced on him by his opponents. While there may be some political maneuvering inherent in Deng's ideological pronouncements in 1985, it should not be forgotten that it was Deng who proposed the four basic principles in the first place, raised the issue of spiritual pollution in 1983, and has always argued that China was building socialism.

Confusion about ideological questions began with a special commentator's article that appeared in *Renmin Ribao* on December 7, 1984, which stated that the works of Marx and Engels could not solve China's problems today. This was quickly corrected on December 10 to say that the works of Marx and Engels could not solve *all* of China's problems today.[9]

Even with the correction to the December 7 commentary, a more liberal ideological atmosphere continued into 1985. At the Fourth Congress of the Chinese Writers Association, rising political star Hu Qili encouraged writers to say what they think, demanding "the freedom of literary and art creation." Yet Hu also warned that this freedom was to be used to serve reform. Decadent bourgeois ideas were not part of this artistic freedom.[10]

On January 1, 1985, a small booklet of Deng Xiaoping's writings from September 1, 1982 to November 1, 1984 was released, under the title *Build Socialism with Chinese Characteristics*. Much of the content of this work dealt with China's open door policy, the Hong Kong and Taiwan questions, and the reform program. But a number of the writings repeated that Marxism had to be sinicized and that China was building socialism with Chinese characteristics. Deng conceded that some veteran officials worried that the open door policy might lead to the restoration of capitalism. But Deng assured them that although the open policy might introduce some negative factors, the restoration of capitalism was impossible.[11]

Yet Deng and other commentators on ideological questions failed to provide much in the way of content for Chinese socialism. To be sure, they repeatedly mentioned increasing China's output and preventing polarization of wealth as some got rich before others, but a compelling ideological vision that might appeal to the Chinese people or the CCP was not articulated. Idealistic appeals were unpersuasive because the ideals of the Party leadership were quite vague. The regime has been unable to formulate a set of broad ideological principles, or even convene an often mentioned national conference on ideology to discuss them. Even in Deng's case, after a brief round of publicity in January 1985, references to *Build Socialism with Chinese Characteristics* have declined drastically.

Shortly after the publication of *Build Socialism*, Deng and Hu Yaobang began to reconsider some of the recent ideological statements of the regime. Deng's seeming confidence that capitalism posed no danger to the regime was rethought, and the apparent freedom of creation Hu Qili applied to writers was limited. Thus, in a speech to journalists in February, which was published in April, Hu Yaobang told journalists they should not copy the slogan "freedom of creation," and that Party journalists should be mouthpieces of the Party. He argued that Chinese journalists had nothing to learn from western societies about freedom of the press. In his speech Hu took pains to point out that central authorities have consistently upheld opposition to decadent and moribund capitalist ideas, and that Deng had particularly pointed this out in his talks on ideological work, especially in his speech to the Second Plenum of the Twelfth Central Committee.[12] It was this speech of Deng's that raised the issue of "spiritual pollution". Nor did Hu say that the campaign against spiritual pollution was wrong, only that the Party Secretariat and the State Council had failed to exert adequate guidance over it. It is true that Chinese communism places journalism in a different category of activity than literature and art, demanding greater conformity from reporters and editors, but Hu seemed to present a particularly hard line.

Deng, too, began to reemphasize ideological goals. At the National Science Conference, which discussed the reform of the science and technology management system, he urged people to have "lofty ideals, moral integrity, education, and a sense of discipline." It was particularly important, he argued, that lofty ideals and a sense of discipline be stressed at the present time. Moreover, he said, "Some people are worried that China will turn capitalist. You cannot say that they are worried for nothing. We should use facts, not empty words, to dispel this worry and answer those who really hope us to turn capitalist."[13] Thus, Deng back-tracked from his earlier view that the open policy could not bring about capitalist restoration. He was still confident that capitalism could not be restored in China, but he was now willing to concede that this idea had some merit and had to be refuted concretely. Deng's chosen audience for these pronouncements is also significant. If any group is likely to have suffered inordinately from ideology in the past, or is not likely to be particularly interested in ideology at present, it is Chinese scientists and technical experts, and intellectuals more generally. Yet it is precisely this group which Deng chose to hear his reemphasis on more ideological themes.

By June and early July, Deng was prepared to label the newly established special economic zones "experiments." "We hope they will succeed. But if it [the special economic zone policy] fails, we can draw lessons from it."[14] His talks on the special zones in *Build Socialism* evinced no sense that Shenzhen and other special zones were experiments.[15] Deng was still confident that the zones would succeed, but his backing for them was no longer as unequivocal as it had been. Surely the failure of Shenzhen to perform as expected and the repeated cases of corruption uncovered there forced him to retreat on this point. In any event, Deng was partially distancing himself from a policy he had favored since 1978. In other, broader terms, he implicitly admitted that there were minimum standards of "socialism" that had to be met by the reforms. The uninhibited capitalism of the special economic zones was at the borderline of the ideologically acceptable.

Deng's concern with ideological themes continued into September, in his speech to the Party Conference. But we will consider that speech in connection with the other developments associated with that conclave. Suffice it to say here that throughout 1985 Deng and other reformers were increasingly concerned about ideological issues. They agreed that ideological and moral education should be strengthened to limit the effect of the decadent influences introduced by the open door policy. They also seemed to imply that ideology was still important in evaluating the progress China was making under the reforms, and as a guide for "correct behavior." In short, they seemed to be arguing that ideology deserved a higher place on the political agenda, and during 1985, their views on ideological questions appeared more restrictive than they had been in 1984.

Transforming the Leadership

Throughout 1985, the leadership of the Chinese Communist Party was revivified. Younger, more competent cadres who favored reform replaced more senior political figures. Some of those replaced clearly were political conservatives. In other cases, the change-over in leadership reflected attempts to institute, or regularize, a system of retirement and promotion. Whatever the reason, by the end of the year Deng and his allies could be well pleased with their efforts. Leaders at all levels of the political system were increasingly cut from reformist cloth.

In most general terms, the highlight of leadership transformation was the cultivation of the "third echelon" of leaders. This group was young by Chinese political standards—mostly in their early 50s—and with at least some higher education. It was to be groomed to be "the next generation" of Party leadership. Not coincidentally, the promotion of this group was designed to insure that reform was institutionalized in the leadership, and would not end with Deng Xiaoping's death.

The first stage in the development of the third line of leadership occurred in late April, when 1,000 young and middle aged leaders were singled out for rapid advancement at the central level. Shortly thereafter, the Party decided to put 30,000 younger cadres at the provincial and prefectural levels on the "fast track." An additional 100,000 younger leaders were to take on leading positions at the county level.[16]

In addition to the advance of the younger generation as a whole, a number of individual personnel moves attracted wide attention. Of greatest note, the long-time commander of the Northeast Military Region, Li Desheng, was removed from that post, and later in the year from the Politburo. Li is thought to have had mixed feelings about the reforms, and he ran Manchuria according to his own ideas. Similarly, Deng Liqun was removed from his post as head of the Party Propaganda Department. Deng Liqun was the point man in the drive against spiritual pollution in late 1983, and had shown himself to be a conservative on ideological issues. But despite his loss of control over the Propaganda Department (he was replaced by the relatively unknown Zhu Houze), Deng Liqun retained his seat on the Party Secretariat, maintaining his influence over propaganda issues from there. Finally, in a perhaps less politically motivated move, Wang Hai replaced Politburo member Zhang Tingfa as commander of the Chinese Air Force. Zhang lost his politburo seat in September.[17]

But the real shake-up in the leadership came at the 4th and 5th Plenums of the 12th Central Committee and the National Party Conference, all held in September 1985. At the 4th Plenum, 131 members of the Politburo, the Central Committee, the Discipline Inspection Commission, and the Advisory Commission resigned. Most significantly, 10 of the 24 members of the Politburo and about 20 percent of the Central Committee stepped down. In a number of cases, the resignations were entirely voluntary. In others, Deng Xiaoping probably pushed people out. The net result of these retirements was that military representation on the Politburo (and the Central Committee) dropped significantly, from 40 to 18 percent, and the average age of the Politburo declined from about 77, as Ye Jianying and others in their 80s and 70s left the political stage, to about 70 in the new Politburo.

At the 5th Plenum, which followed the 4th Plenum and the Party Conference (where proposals for the 7th Five Year Plan were presented and new Central Committee members were chosen), new members of the Politburo were selected. Yao Yilin was promoted from alternate member of the Politburo to full member, and Wu Xuegian, Qiao Shi, Li Peng, Tian Jiyun, and Hu Qili were all made full members of the Politburo. Most observers see Qiao, Li, Tian, and particularly Hu Qili as China's top leaders of the future. The Party Secretariat also saw significant changes as a number of members of the third echelon were added to its ranks as well. Fifty-six full members (some promoted from alternate status) and 35 new alternates were elected to the Central Committee. Many of these new leaders were college educated and the average age of this group was just over 50.[18]

Thus, seemingly without a great deal of opposition, Deng Xiaoping was able to further entrench his supporters in the Chinese leadership. On balance, it is safe to say that the changeover in personnel will give additional impetus to reform efforts in China. In particular, the Party Secretariat seems to be the stronghold of reformers. But the attitudes of a number of key officials are sufficiently vague or subject to change that a firm weighting of the political forces at the top is not possible. The personnel aspects of the Party meetings in September do not appear to have generated a great deal of political conflict. A number of older leaders may have wished to retain power; in the end, however, they went along with Deng's plan. But at this moment of victory for Deng and the reform forces in the leadership, many things began to go seriously awry. One of these problem areas concerned not who was being promoted, but *how* the new leadership was being promoted. Indeed, half a dozen major problems or sources of opposition began to coalesce in the second half of 1985.

Problems and Opposition

By this time, problems with the reform program and other policies were generating political opposition. The sources of this opposition varied from issue to issue, and the voices of opposition do not appear to have united against the entire reform program. It is impossible to say how widespread and deep discontent with the present situation is. However, it is clear that the leadership is well aware of its problems and is quite concerned about them.

Among the major problem areas that created ill feelings between the leadership and society were the overheated economy, inflation, corruption (particularly related to the open door policy), student dissatisfaction (stemming from a variety of sources), ethnic minority discontent, urban dissatisfaction with price reform, and opposition within the Party itself. By the end of the year, perhaps for the first time since reform was launched, the leadership could not be sure that the populace was behind the reform efforts.

Throughout the first half of 1985, the Chinese economy was overheated. The growth rate between January and July exceeded 20 percent, greatly overstretching infrastructural facilities and state supplies. The People's Bank was lending out too much money, so that too much was circulating.

All these factors contributed to inflationary pressures. Moreover, the boom psychology among economic decision-makers was counter-productive to true reforms. Factory managers were so busy chasing after scarce factors of production that efficiency concerns declined in salience. Thus in 1985, repeating a familiar pattern in the post-Mao era, large surges in investment followed significant policy pronouncements. This particular surge was the product of the autumn 1984 decision to reform the urban economy. However, the boom itself actually slowed reform efforts.[19] The price reform measures announced in the first half of 1985 also contributed to inflationary pressures. This, in turn, led to dissatisfaction on the part of urban residents. Even the government-run journal *Beijing Review* contained the following passage illustrating problems with the price reform program:

> "Never have I seen such large-scale price rises since liberation. It's terrible," complained an elderly man. . . . "I don't think I can maintain or improve my standard of living, as some officials have promised. This 7.50 yuan subsidy will not make up for my loss in the price rise," he said.[20]

Similar reports appeared elsewhere. The *Los Angeles Times* quoted one Chinese woman as saying "My mother says that 10 years ago China was in chaos, but Mao kept prices stable. She says now China is stable, but prices are in chaos."[21] Apparently, inflation was such a political problem that the CCP announced that no new price reform efforts would be launched in 1986.[22] This, of course, would only delay true economic reform.

A second economic policy area that created problems for the elite was the question of the open door policy, the huge corruption scandal that occurred on Hainan Island, and the problem of corruption more broadly. On foreign trade policy in general, there was elite consensus. China ran a very large foreign trade deficit in 1985. Chinese leaders argued that too many consumer goods and automobiles were being imported, and most agreed that too much control had been lost in the foreign trade sector.

While there was a consensus about regaining more control over the import sector, other aspects of the open door policy became more controversial. Thus, in July, the Chinese announced that plans to open up 10 of 14 major coastal cities had to be put on hold for the time being. This did not mean these cities were closed to trade, but rather that investments required to make them especially desirable to foreign investors were not likely to be forthcoming. Thus, a policy on which Deng Xiaoping staked a great amount of his prestige in 1984 was coming partially undone in 1985.[23]

Similarly, the Special Economic Zones also became highly controversial. While it was true that the zones, particularly Shenzhen, the largest, had grown spectacularly, the benefits obtained were much less than expected. China had expended far more capital building up the infrastructure of the zones than it had gained in foreign exchange. Moreover, the vast majority of production in Shenzhen was being sold in China, not exported abroad. Corruption also seemed to be endemic in the zones. By late 1985, it appeared that the leadership had decided the zones would have to be more self-sufficient. Although the zones would remain open, the state was not going to provide them with many more resources. Apparently some Chinese leaders had greatly overstated the benefits to be derived from the zones. By late 1985, a more sober attitude towards the zones was in evidence.[24]

A final problem with the open door was the massive Hainan Island corruption scandal, a vivid example of the more generalized phenomenon of outside influences entering China through the open door, promoting widespread corruption in the Party. The Hainan case was the worst of many instances of Party cadres engaging in illegal business practices. More than 89,000 cars and trucks as well as other expensive consumer goods were imported through Hainan and resold on the mainland. Almost all government, Party, and military units on Hainan were involved in these activities.[25] Conservative Party leaders pointed to this and other incidents as the costs of the open door policy, and some of these leaders were apparently willing to see the door closed again.

While Deng and his allies did not agree to this, they were clearly concerned about the increasingly rampant corruption.

Even before the corruption scandals specifically related to the open door emerged, growing corruption within the Party on a more general level had been noted and attacked. Thus, in early March, the head of the State Administration for Industry and Commerce noted that Party and government departments had opened up more than 16,000 businesses nationwide. He implied that these businesses were an invitation for corruption. Similarly, Bo Yibo, the head of the Party's Commission for Guiding Party Rectification, warned against the development of "new unhealthy tendencies" which included cadres (or their families) engaging in business, illegal resales of imports and foreign exchange, arbitrary raising of prices, private use of public property and funds, and other types of activities that led to private gains at the expense of the state.[26] By early 1986, the situation was so bad that a third Party organization was created to supplement the drive against corruption in the Party. In addition to the Discipline Inspection Commission, and the Commission Guiding Party Rectification, a new *ad hoc* group was created to deal with corruption.[27] In contradistinction to the two other bodies, the *ad hoc* group was clearly controlled by the reformers. What all this suggests is that the problem of corruption is now so severe that the Party leadership, be it conservative or reformist, cannot count on the Party and state structure to carry out Party policy reliably. In other words, the organizational weapon is so decayed that Party leaders can no longer trust the Party to carry out its missions.

Besides problems related to the economy, the open door, and corruption, more overt challenges to the Party developed in 1985 as well. Sectors of society, particularly students, and members of the Party itself questioned the evolution of the reform program. Each source of opposition will be considered in turn.

Public protest was a common occurrence in 1985. In April, youths sent down to the countryside demanded that they be allowed to return to Beijing. In May, a near riot developed as disgruntled Chinese soccer fans turned their frustrations on foreigners and others after the Chinese national team lost an important match to Hong Kong. Throughout the fall, students rallied to protest a variety of policies including aspects of Sino-Japanese relations, the open door policy, special privileges for the sons and daughters of Party leaders, and poor living conditions in colleges. Finally, in December, minority students from Xinjiang studying in Beijing protested against nuclear testing in Xinjiang. Many of these protests were repeated in other areas of China, though the situation in Beijing is the best documented.

Several important points should be made about these instances of popular protest. First, with the possible exception of the soccer riot, the authorities responded in a relatively calm and non-violent way. Party leaders met with the aggrieved parties and tried to persuade them of the correctness of the Party's policies. The emphasis was on persuasion, not coercion. This may bode well for future efforts to reform the political system.

The student protest must have been particularly worrisome for the leadership however. College students were, after all, perhaps the social group with the most to gain from the open door policy. They benefited from improved job prospects, access to new forms of learning, and the chance to study abroad. Despite this, some Chinese students apparently believed that the open door was flawed for several reasons. First, they felt that too much of China's sovereignty was being sacrificed to open the door. This was particularly the case with Sino-Japanese relations. Thus, in this instance, students acted out of patriotic motives, powerfully reinforced by the Party's own propaganda celebrating the fortieth anniversary of the end of the war against Japan. Second, the students also seemed to believe that the sons and daughters of the elite were monopolizing the chances to study abroad and gain access to desirable positions after graduation. Thus, the open door was perhaps viewed as something of a chimera, from which only the well-connected could profit. Student demands stemming from this view might be quite hostile to the existing political system. Perhaps only true democratic reforms would make the open door fair for all.

These views and the more particularistic causes for student protest, such as bad food in school cafeterias, left the Party with another major problem. Educated young people were essential to make the reform program work. Only they could provide the skills needed to modernize China. They were the logical constituency gaining from reform. Yet, a significant segment of this group which had the most to gain from the reforms appeared to be hostile to at least some parts of the reformist program. What could be done about the disaffection felt by this critical group? Moreover, the discontent of this group who benefited rather directly from reform might well lead Party leaders to wonder uneasily about the attitudes of other elements of society who were not profiting so directly from the reform program. At the very least, the student protests suggested that the link between the state and society was weaker than the Party had assumed.

Finally, Deng and his allies faced a number of challenges from within the Party itself. Some of these were more direct than others, but there were many straws in the wind showing that the reform program was in political trouble.

Thus, in a possibly allegorical article, a historian writing on the failure of the "100 Days of Reform in 1898" argued that "one of the main reasons for the failure of the reform movement was precisely that the pace of the reform movement had been too fast." The article also noted that the ideals of the reformers "were seriously divorced from reality" and that "their theories about reform were not convincing."[28] If this article was not part of an attack on the reformers, other materials published in November 1985 were clearly counter to the spirit of reform. In an article commemorating the 30th anniversary of the Chinese nuclear industry and the rapid development of China's hydrogen bomb, a former minister argued "Whether in the field of advanced defense technology or in the basic industries, foreigners do not let us learn their confidential information."[29] If foreigners were not going to share their advanced technology in basic industries, what was the purpose of the open door, this article seemed to ask.

Another area where the reformers may have gotten into trouble concerned the selection of the third echelon. Hong Kong journals with contacts in China claimed that the rising stars in the Chinese political system seemed to come from three basic groups. These were the "princes group," "the secretaries group," and the "Communist Youth League group." The princes group referred to sons and daughters of the top elite who were inheriting their parents' positions. For example, Li Tieying, the Minister of Electronics, is the son of revolutionary veteran Li Weihan; Ding Henggao, the chairman of the National Defense Science and Technology Industry Commission, is the son-in-law of Marshal Nie Rongzhen, and Zou Jiahua, the Minister of the Ordinance Industry, is the son-in-law of Marshal Ye Jianying.[30] Many other examples could be cited. The secretaries group was made up of people who had served as secretaries for major political figures and who were now holding independent positions. Tian Jiyun appears to be an example of this kind of leader. Finally, there is a group of younger leaders who have risen first through the Communist Youth League and then into the central leadership. Hu Qili is the best example here.

While the people associated with these groups may all be quite competent, the process of their selection raises serious questions. A nepotistic, factional pattern of selection and advancement appears to characterize the development of the third echelon. Party credibility about the abilities of the third line of leadership is not enhanced when it is learned that many of the younger generation of leaders are inheriting their positions from their parents. The elite appears to be closed, and talent, arguably, plays only a limited role in promotion. This is likely to spawn resentment both within the Party and in society at large.

Finally, Deng and his allies face difficulties at the very top of the Party hierarchy. At the Party Conference in September 1985, the speeches of Deng Xiaoping and Chen Yun revealed significant differences in emphasis, as well as many areas of agreement.

The conventional wisdom about these speeches is that Chen opposed Deng's reform efforts, while Deng, in a somewhat muted form, defended the reforms.[31] Chen upheld the primacy of the planned economy, whereas Deng only argued that the state-owned sector of the economy should be dominant. Chen argued for more control over grain production, which Deng largely ignored. Chen may also have criticized Deng for acting too arbitrarily. Chen also argued for much greater attention to ideological issues, fighting corruption, and demanding high morals from members of the Party. Yet Deng too stressed ideological education and the purity of Party members. Both seemed to agree on promoting the third echelon. They agreed that reforms should proceed cautiously and that the rate of economic growth in the 7th Five Year Plan should not be excessive.

Many observers emphasize the points of difference between Chen and Deng and suggest that Chen's views are characteristic of those who resist reform. There is no denying there are some disagreements between the two, but for the most part, they are capable of working together, and a major Party split is not imminent. What the two speeches do indicate is that there are different understandings of what constitutes reform, and that until a more unified view of reform comes into existence, the coalition dominating Chinese politics right now is a fragile one. In other words, Chen Yun and his allies are not opposed to reform. Rather, they represent what might be called the moderate reform position in the Chinese political spectrum. They were committed to reform policies up to the fall of 1984, but currently they seem less interested in pressing forward with major new reforms, and more concerned with refining the existing reform policies. In contrast to the moderate reformers are the radical reformers. Nominally headed by Deng, but perhaps best represented by Hu Yaobang and Hu Qili, this group sees all the previous reforms as merely preparing the foundation for fundamental reforms of the economic and political system.[32]

By the end of 1985, there were signs of substantial resistance to certain aspects of reforms from many elements of society and from within the Party. Economic conditions, the difficulty of instituting new prices, and other objective factors contributed to the development of discontent. But by the end of the year it was apparent that a significant segment of the political system had doubts about the reform program, or at least parts of it, and that in 1986 substantial reforms are not likely to be on the political agenda.

Conclusion

The Chinese leadership faces many difficult problems in 1986. China ran a large trade deficit in 1985, and the price of its principal export commodity, oil, has dropped in value by approximately 50 percent. The grain harvest declined by 30 million tons, just when Chinese agricultural exports were beginning to make significant inroads in important markets. Another of China's major exports, textiles, faces growing protectionism in advanced industrial economies. In short, the Chinese economy will face stringent conditions in 1986.

Coupled with this lack of flexibility in its economic relations with the world, the leadership faces a number of difficult domestic political issues. In the early stages of the reform program, the Party was able to marshal significant public support, particularly in the rural sector. But by the end of 1985, the degree of public support for further reforms in the urban sector was uncertain. Price increases for basic commodities led a wide segment of the urban population to grumble about the Party's handling of the economy. Students more actively criticized the Party's open door policy and other initiatives. The Party itself appeared split and/or anxious to profit from the opportunities inherent in the reform program at the expense of Party obligations.

Prior to 1984, when Deng faced opposition in the Party, he had a social constituency he could count on. Now, it is not clear that such a constituency exists in the urban areas. Moreover, it seems safe to say that the Party is not much more united or capable today than it was several years ago. The reformers are therefore confronted by a fundamental dilemma: how to continue reform without overwhelming public support for it and when the bureaucratic instruments for implementing reform policies are themselves in various stages of disrepair.

Because of this dilemma, Deng et al., are likely to spend the bulk of 1986 consolidating reforms already enacted, accumulating strength for future efforts, and trying to regain the support of society. How they will be able to accomplish this last task is unclear. But given the skill with which the reformers have kept reform on the political agenda since 1978, it would be a mistake to argue that reform is dead. New reforms in 1986 are unlikely, but with careful nurturing, reform will continue.

Notes

My thanks to Ann Fenwick, Harry Harding, Deborah Kwittken, and Lynn White for helpful comments on an earlier draft of this paper.

1. See Thomas P. Bernstein, "Domestic Politics," in Steven M. Goldstein, ed., *China Briefing, 1984* (Boulder: Westview Press, 1985), pp. 1–19.

2. I take this phrase from John W. Lewis, "The Social Limits of Politically Induced Change," in Chandler Morse et al., *Modernization by Design* (Ithaca: Cornell University Press, 1969), pp. 1–33. However, the analysis here differs somewhat from the theoretical discussion found in Lewis.

3. See *Foreign Broadcast Information Service, Daily Report, China* [hereafter, FBIS], March 21, 1985, K1-K9, for a text of the document. See Richard Suttmeier's chapter in this volume for a more thorough discussion.

4. FBIS, May 30, 1985, K1-K11. For a much fuller discussion, see Peter Seybolt's contribution to this volume.

5. See, for example, *Beijing Review* [hereafter BR], January 7, 1985, p. 15; January 28, 1985, pp. 16–19, 24; February 18, 1985, pp. 16–18, 29; and February 10, 1986, pp. III-XV. Barry Naughton discusses these policies in more detail in his chapter.

6. See FBIS, March 4, 1985, K1-K10, BR, April 9, 1985, pp. 8–9.

7. BR, June 17, 1985, p. 6; *New York Times* [hereafter NYT], June 11 and 23, 1985; and *Christian Science Monitor* [hereafter CSM], June 21, 1985.

8. On the turbine sales, see *International Herald Tribune*, August 10–11, 1985. On the other sales or proposed deals, see NYT, January 27, 1986.

9. See *Renmin Ribao*, December 7, 1984 and December 10, 1984

10. FBIS, December 31, 1984, K4-K8.

11. Deng, *Build Socialism with Chinese Characteristics* (Beijing: Foreign Languages Press, 1985), p. 62.

12. Hu's speech is in FBIS, April 15, 1985, K1-K15.

13. See FBIS, March 11, 1985, K5-K6.

14. BR, July 15, 1985, p. 6.

15. Deng, *supra* note 11, pp. 25–27.

16. See FBIS, April 29, 1985, K5-K6. See also Richard Baum, "China in 1985: The Greening of the Revolution," *Asian Survey*, Vol.XXVI, No.1, (January 1986), pp. 30–53, especially pp. 32–36.

17. See FBIS, July 8, 1985, W4-W8; July 12, K15; July 29, K4; and September 23, K7.

18. See FBIS, September 23, K2 and K7; FEER, September 26, 1985, pp. 18–19; FEER, October 3, 1985, pp. 10–12, BR, September 30, 1985, p. 7; and Baum, *supra* note 16, pp. 34–36.

19. Problems with the economy are discussed briefly in Chen Yun and Zhao Ziyang's speeches to the Party meetings in September 1985. See BR, September 30, 1985, pp. 18–20, especially p. 19, and BR, October 7, 1985, pp. I-V, especially p. II.

20. BR, May 20, 1985, p. 7.

21. *Los Angeles Times*, February 4, 1985, cited in Baum, *supra* note 16, p.44, n. 64.

22. See BR, February 10, 1986, pp. VII-X.

23. See FEER, July 25, 1985, p. 10. On Deng's stake, see *Build Socialism, supra* note 11, p. 56.

24. See, for example, BR, September 30, 1985, pp. 4–5 and FBIS, August 7, 1985, W1-W8. For general background on the zones, suggesting a number of their structural problems, see Ann Fenwick, "Evaluating China's Special Economic Zones," *International Tax and Business Lawyer*, Vol. 2, (Fall 1984), pp. 376–397.

25. See, for example, CSM, August 6, 1985; *International Herald Tribune*, August 24–25, 1985; and NYT, December 13, 1985.

26. FBIS, March 12, 1985, K2-K3, and FBIS, March 14, K1-K8. Many other reports could be cited.

27. FEER, January 30, 1986, pp. 22–24.

28. FBIS, November 5, 1985, K1-K4. Quotation from K1.

29. FBIS, November 14, 1985, K7-K11; see K10.

30. See *China Trade Report*, November 1985, p. 10.

31. Texts of the speeches are found in FBIS, September 23, 1985, K8-K13 for Deng, K13-K16 for Chen. Interpretations of these speeches are found in FEER, October 3, 1985, pp. 10–12; NYT, September 24, 1985; and CSM, September 24, 1985. For a view that emphasizes the similarity between Chen and Deng, see David Bachman, "Differing Visions of China's Post-Mao Economy: The Ideas of Chen Yun, Deng Xiaoping, and Zhao Ziyang," *Asian Survey*, March 1986, pp. 292–321.

32. I am greatly indebted to Harry Harding and Kenneth Lieberthal for these ideas on the moderate and radical reformers.

2 Foreign Relations

Michael B. Yahuda

China's self-proclaimed independent foreign policy[1] that had been developed since 1982 continued to serve China well throughout most of 1985. It facilitated the expansion of more variegated sets of relationships with all parts of the world and it enabled China, for example, to intensify its participation in the (Western) international economic system while simultaneously strengthening its economic ties with the Soviet Union and the countries of Eastern Europe. The independent foreign policy may be seen as designed to bring about a more peaceful international environment in which China can concentrate its efforts on domestic modernization. However, because of its relative weakness China's capacity to manoeuvre independently between the two superpowers is dependent upon the character of their bilateral relations and upon their respective policies towards China. Thus China's leaders were re-evaluating aspects of their foreign policy, firstly because of the possibility that in the wake of the November summit meeting the two superpowers may move away from confrontation towards a degree of cooperation in arms control at least; and secondly, because of their failure to convince the Soviet Union that China was truly independent of the United States.

This raised the question as to whether in the long term China has the capacity to sustain an effective independent foreign policy? Or will it be forced to choose between one superpower and another?

A related but separate issue concerning China's foreign policy arises from the problems involved in becoming more economically interdependent with the outside world. Two aspects of this in particular deserve scrutiny: First, will this have a disintegrative effect on domestic Chinese politics as some regions and industries develop much stronger external ties than others and as central ideological and political controls weaken? Second, will it be possible to sustain an independent geopolitical position as China's economic ties with the Western world deepen and become increasingly interlocked? Although these may be seen as questions for the long term the eruption of student demonstrations in the latter part of the year linked domestic discontent with opposition to Japan and showed that already the domestic politics of economic reform were becoming enmeshed with external economic policy. This suggested new ways in which the open door policy, deemed essential to the modernization program, could be threatened by urban discontent with some of the consequences of domestic reform—especially if discontented city dwellers were supported by higher leaders.[2]

Although neither development, in superpower relations or in the politics of economic interdependency, seemed likely to undermine the main directions of China's policy, they attested once again to the greater degree of volatility inherent in China's foreign policy as compared to those of the other major powers. They also pointed up the principal sources of that volatility: Firstly, perceived changes in superpower relations; and secondly, shifts in domestic politics.

China's Independent Foreign Policy

This policy was first developed in 1982 to replace the anti-Soviet orientation of the previous ten years. By the early 1980s China's leaders argued that the international situation and China's place within it had changed. They felt that under the leadership of President Reagan the United States had re-established a rough strategic equilibrium with the Soviet Union. Meanwhile the latter's expansionist phase of the late 1970s had been halted by a combination of pressure from the United States, a preoccupation with Poland and Afghanistan and increasing difficulties because of a sluggish economy. This also meant that the immediate Soviet threat to China had greatly diminished. Moreover, the previous policy of close alignment with the United States in an anti-Soviet coalition had damaged China's reputation with the Third World.

Given the critical importance China's leaders placed on economic development the reduction of tensions with the Soviet Union had great appeal. Indeed, one aspect of the new independent foreign policy stressed the pursuit of a peaceful international environment in which China could focus on domestic modernization.

The practical consequences of the new policy were firstly, a relative distancing of relations with the United States which also facilitated an improvement of Sino-Soviet relations; secondly, a renewed emphasis on Third World themes and Third World relations; and thirdly, an even greater emphasis upon policies that served the interests of the modernization of the Chinese economy.

Deng Xiaoping described the new policy succinctly to the visiting Brazilian President on May 29, 1984.

> China's foreign policy is independent and truly non-aligned. China does not align itself with any country, but invariably pursues a policy of independence. It will not play the United States card or the Soviet Union card. Nor will it allow others to play the China Card. China's foreign policy aims at world peace. With that aim in mind we are wholeheartedly devoted to the modernization program to develop our country and to build socialism with Chinese characteristics.[3]

In fact China was more aligned than this and similar expositions suggested. An unspoken Western tilt has continued to characterize China's foreign relations. Despite Chinese criticisms of America as a superpower that practices hegemonic policies in Central America, the Middle East and other areas distant from China (apart from the question of Taiwan) Chinese and American policies in the Asia-Pacific region closely parallel each other; and in practice China has continued to rely upon the United States as a counter-weight to Soviet military forces in that region. Thus China in effect does not question the American-Japanese security treaty, nor does it oppose the presence of American bases in the Philippines. Sino-American policies towards the Korean peninsula are not irreconcilable, and the two powers follow closely parallel policies in Indochina where they are both in effect allies of Thailand and suppliers of aid to the Khmer Resistance forces. Similarly, with regard to Afghanistan they are both allied with Pakistan and assist the Afghani resistance fighters. Indeed, on the strategic questions that really affect China's security in its immediate region, it is difficult to identify major points of conflict between China and the United States other than the special question of Taiwan.

By contrast, China's criticisms of the Soviet Union focus on the continued invasion of Afghanistan, the backing of Vietnam's military occupation of Cambodia, and the high level of Soviet military deployments near the Chinese border from Xinjiang through Mongolia to the Soviet Far East. These three have been portrayed as the three major obstacles to the normalization of Sino-Soviet relations. In other words, Soviet policies in these areas are regarded as directly threatening China's security. Nevertheless, Sino-Soviet tensions have been gradually reduced as trade and other exchanges have developed.

In a sense the independent foreign policy has served China very well as China was able to retain the strategic and economic benefits of the ties with the West while simultaneously improving relations with Russia and the East Europeans. Additionally China was able to re-develop its third world credentials and more generally develop a complex and variegated diplomacy with all parts of the world.

However, the Geneva Summit in November between General Secretary Gorbachev and President Reagan, with its promise of further meetings and the prospect of possible arms control agreements, has raised new problems for China's leaders. A less confrontational relationship between the two superpowers may diminish China's room to maneuver between them and it may reduce China's strategic significance to the United States.

China and the Strategic Triangle

Although China's leaders went out of their way to de-emphasize the tripartite aspect of China's relations with the Soviet Union and the United States, there can be little doubt that China's relations with the two superpowers have not been conducted as two unconnected sets of bilateral relations. Hu Yaobang conceded the point when in September 1984 he revealed that the Soviet leaders had been told that "China is not entering, and will never enter, into any alliance with the United States against the USSR," and he went on to comment that "the Soviets do not have a correct assessment of the relations between China and the United States."[4] Nevertheless by the end of 1984 Sino-Soviet relations had improved considerably in terms of increased trade and cultural, scientific, and sporting exchanges. In 1982 there began a series of twice yearly consultation meetings between deputy foreign ministers. Trade and cross-border trade began to expand. Following a meeting between the two foreign ministers at the UN in September 1984 (the highest level such meeting for 15 years) Vice Chairman of the Council of Ministers L. Arkhopov visited China in December 1984—the first Soviet official of his level to pay an official visit to China for 25 years. It was agreed to raise the value of trade by 30% from that originally scheduled so as to reach $1.6 billion. The senior leader Chen Yun was moved to note that even if the other major obstacles to normalization were not removed the two "could [still] improve and expand their relations on other matters."[5]

However it was not until Chernenko's death and his replacement as General Secretary of the CPSU by Gorbachev that the momentum of relations picked up. The Russian-speaking rising star Vice Premier Li Peng attended the funeral. Even before his arrival, Gorbachev in a major address to his Party's Central Committee expressed hope for major improvements in Sino-Soviet relations. Li endorsed that and officially described the two great neighbors as "socialist countries." He went on to repeat that China was non-aligned and had no strategic relations with other countries (i.e. the United States). Both Li and Gorbachev expressed their desire to make significant improvements in Sino-Soviet relations.

The following month, in an interview published only in Hong Kong, Hu Yaobang went so far as to appear to dilute China's stand on the three major obstacles. He was quoted as saying that China adhered to only "two" principles: "1) The unstable factors along the borders, namely the obstacles to the security of relevant countries must be removed; and 2) Our country would adhere to its foreign policy of maintaining independence and keeping the initiative in its own hands and would never attach itself to any country or group of countries nor form an alliance with any other country."[6] The interview led to a flurry of speculation that was further fueled by a reported remark of Deng Xiaoping. Allegedly he expressed willingness to arrange a summit meeting with the new Soviet leadership if it would give way on only one of the obstacles. But in the absence of a concessionary response from the Soviet side, China's leaders reverted to the standard formula of the three obstacles. Hu was later quoted as having remarked that "improvement of relations cannot be determined by the desire of only one side."[7] That indeed is one of the major problems in the development of the independent foreign policy.

Meanwhile in an interview with New Zealand journalists on the eve of leaving on a tour of the South Pacific in April, Hu Yaobang not only affirmed his support for New Zealand's ban of port visits by nuclear and nuclear armed American ships, but went on to declare that China took the same view too. For strategic reasons the United States has consistently refused to reveal which of its ships are or are not armed with nuclear weapons. The New Zealand government was aware that by denying admission to its ports by U.S. nuclear vessels it was in effect denying admission to all U.S. naval vessels. It is not known whether Hu was fully aware of the consequences of his remarks, but they led to the indefinite postponement of the first official visit to Chinese ports by U.S. Naval vessels since 1949. The visits had been agreed on earlier during high level military exchanges between China and the United States.

Although not much attention was paid to the issue by the official Chinese media, it pointed up a major qualitative difference in Sino-American and Sino-Soviet relations. The former involved firstly exchanges of much more senior figures; thus President Reagan's visit to China of 1984 was reciprocated in July 1985 by a visit by China's President Li Xiannian and a large entourage that also included Vice Premier Li Peng, whereas Sino-Soviet relations did not rise above Vice Premier level. Secondly the exchanges also included senior military personnel and an enormous range of people from virtually all the major organizations involved in Sino-American relations, whereas those of Sino-Soviet relations excluded the military and the other exchanges, though growing, were very small by comparison. Thirdly, the volume of trade, investment, technology transfers, etc. bore no comparison. Despite Chinese complaints about limitations and delays on Sino-American trade its value in 1985 grew to $7.7 billion from $6 billion in 1984.[8] In other words the value of its growth exceeded the $1.6 billion total of Sino-Soviet trade for the year. The United States ranked third as China's trading partner and first as investor in China. Fourthly, the United States was freely seen as the most important country in sustaining China's open door policies.

If the "three issues" in Sino-Soviet relations were obstacles to normalization, those in Sino-American relations were more in the nature of irritants. The most important was Taiwan, which has the potential to become a serious problem indeed. During the American visit of President Li in July and that of Vice President Bush to China in October the Chinese side pressed the issue, but it was noteworthy that the Americans were not specifically accused of breaking the 1982 agreement limiting U.S. arms sales to the island. Deng Xiaoping who is thought to value ties with America more highly than some of his senior colleagues expressed himself on the issue as follows on 1st August:

> We are rather happy with the present Sino-U.S. relations. During his visit to the United States, President Li Xiannian was warmly received. The presence of President Reagan after his operation was a friendly gesture. There is also an obstacle to Sino-U.S. relations, namely, the Taiwan issue. They say that they do not interfere and that they are not involved. We are of the opinion that the United States has always interfered and has always been involved in the Taiwan issue. They have never stopped interfering. The United States can facilitate a dialogue across the strait and can contribute to the early peaceful reunification of China.[9]

At other times China's leaders including Deng have hinted darkly that there were influential circles in the U.S. who viewed Taiwan as a strategic asset ("an unsinkable aircraft carrier") and still others who coveted it for other reasons. However, the interesting point about Deng's remarks is that he did not simply want the United States to stand aside in a passive way but he wanted it, in effect, to put pressure on the government in Taiwan to negotiate with Beijing.

The other major irritants in Sino-American relations center on trade restrictions and legal obstacles in the release of advanced technology.[10] Some progress was registered on these fronts in 1985: President Reagan duly vetoed the Jenkins protectionist bill, and during President Li's visit to the U.S. the American government accepted, and was able to persuade Congress to accept, a memorandum of official conversations between Vice Premier Li Peng and the American chief negotiator on nuclear exchanges as equivalent to the legal guarantees normally required by Congress before ratifying agreements on nuclear exchanges.

The pace of improvement of Sino-Soviet relations in 1985 in the end flattered only to deceive. Vice Premier Yao Yilin visited the Soviet Union in July and returned with two new long term economic and trade agreements. The two foreign ministers met at the UN on 26–27 September and agreed to exchange visits. Two weeks later a delegation of the Supreme Soviet headed by its Chairman Lev Tolkunov visited China to resume relations with the National People's Congress after a 20-year break. The 7th round of Sino-Soviet consultations issued a joint communique on 20 October registering further progress on the political issues. Overlapping with the visit of U.S. Vice President Bush, Beijing also hosted the Soviet director of the Institute of the U.S.A. and Canada, Georgiy Arbatov, from 11–25 October, presumably to be thoroughly briefed on Soviet views regarding the imminent superpowers summit. The official Xinhua News Agency later quoted him as saying that "the Chinese know clearly that nobody shall be able to stand by with folded arms if a global or Soviet-U.S. nuclear war breaks out."[11] The implication was that because China's leaders did not any longer think they would benefit from a Soviet-American war there was room for narrowing Sino-Soviet differences on global strategic issues.

However, the Chinese response to the Geneva Gorbachev-Reagan summit has been to acknowledge that American-Soviet relations have softened somewhat and to register irritation at the Soviet failure to do something about the three major obstacles. Soviet officials, apparently, have refused to discuss the issues in detail. A Chinese official privately cited considerable dissatisfaction with the attitude of the Soviet Deputy Foreign Minister and senior China specialist M.S. Kapitsa who visited China in December. He was said to have exuded confidence in public about Sino-Soviet relations while refusing to "talk seriously" about the three issues of Afghanistan, Cambodia or border troops. The rapid expansion of Sino-Soviet relations in commercial, cultural, and sporting spheres that has taken place over the last two years coupled with the exchange of high level delegations have led Western diplomats to the view that normalization of relations is taking place without it being formally acknowledged. Perhaps because of this, a spokesman of the Chinese Foreign Ministry went out of his way to reject a Soviet proposal that both sides sign a mutual nonaggression pact. He bluntly stated that: "the proposal that had been put forward for many years has been categorically rejected by the Chinese [side]. We have time and again reiterated that the removal of the three obstacles is the only way to normalize Sino-Soviet relations, because it not only has a bearing on China's security but also on the upholding of international justice."[12]

Despite the success of their diplomacy in improving relations with the Soviet Union without sacrificing their ties with the United States, China's leaders were nevertheless vulnerable to possible changes of policy that either or both of the superpowers might carry out towards China arising out of new understandings that might be forged in the wake of the Geneva Summit. Unnamed Asian and Western diplomats were quoted as suggesting that China's leaders would dwell more publicly on the Soviet failure to budge on the three major obstacles so as implicitly to remind the United States of China's continued role as a counterweight to the Soviet Union.[13] As if to confirm this analysis, Vice-Foreign Minister Qian Qichen, who led the Chinese side in the seven rounds of Sino-Soviet talks begun in 1982, declared at the year's end that although Sino-Soviet relations had improved in recent years in the areas of economics, trade, and technology, political relations, however, had not improved. Blaming the Soviet side he used harsher language than had been used for three years.

> What is inconceivable is that the Soviet Union, while repeatedly expressing the desire to improve relations with China, has tried, under various pretexts, to dodge discussion on ways to remove these obstacles. They agreed to talk about the easing of international tensions and the elimination of regional conflicts, but at the same time show an unwillingness to talk about the Afghanistan and Kampuchean issues. It seems the Soviet side has a misconception that it can get around these obstacles, or that the obstacles will vanish by themselves.[14]

These developments pointed to a fundamental dilemma in China's independent foreign policy. In order to persuade the Russians that China was really not in strategic alignment with the United States against them China's leaders would presumably have to distance themselves still further from the United States. However, to do so would endanger many of the tacit and perhaps covert understandings that exist with America. Moreover it could lead to China being perhaps dangerously exposed and alone while the United States and the Soviet Union might be moving towards areas of cooperation.

Japan and the Open Door

Japan is of critical importance to China in the strategic issues of North East Asia and the Asian Pacific and especially in China's external economic relations. Japan is by far China's most important trading partner, accounting for 25% of the total of China's trade.[15] At the high point of China's policy of building an anti-Soviet coalition, Deng Xiaoping declared in Tokyo in January 1979 that together China and Japan could hold up half of heaven! In the more restrained diplomacy of the independent foreign policy, in 1983 Hu Yaobang established with Japan's Prime Minister Nakasone the "21st Century Committee for Sino-Japanese Friendship" so as to institutionalize a special relationship with Japan that could be passed on to the younger generation. This was a unique arrangement in the history of the international relations of either country.

Although China's policy of the open door brought the two countries closer together it also expanded the numbers of people dealing with Japan (as indeed with all other foreign countries) beyond the small coterie of officials who previously handled foreign relations. Moreover it also brought Japan, along with the rest of the world, into closer interaction with Chinese society at large. The open door has also led to a closer confrontation between China's political and economic values and norms and those associated with the West. Aspects of the open door have become inextricably involved with domestic politics. Thus the decline of collectivist norms, the growth of individualistic sentiments, unabashed consumerism, corruption, increased political indifference and so on is often portrayed as resulting from the spread of capitalistic influences attendant upon the open door. Consequently, those opposed to aspects of the post 1978 reforms have tended to seize upon these issue areas.

Independently of these developments, the period since the death of Mao has witnessed the promotion of patriotism (or nationalism) as a platform on which to appeal to the idealism and loyalty of young people in particular. China's leaders consciously developed this theme at the same time as they began to espouse the independent foreign policy.[16] Chinese nationalism or patriotism was perceived as a more unifying and credible ideological theme on which to galvanize support for the new domestic policies at a time in which socialist orthodoxy had lost its appeal and had been challenged by some of the new policies. But in China, as elsewhere, nationalism can have a negative anti-foreign aspect as well as more positive nation-building aspects.

The two strands of social discontent and patriotism combined together in the last quarter of 1985 to result in student protests that included denunciations of Japan. The link between patriotism and opposition to Japan had been publicly drawn by China's leaders earlier in the summer. Firstly, in the build up to marking the 40th anniversary of Japan's defeat, various cities had mounted exhibitions including accounts of Japanese wartime atrocities. After all, important dimensions of the growth of nationalist consciousness in China in the first half of this century centered on resistance to Japanese incursions into China and the Communist victory itself grew out of the war of resistance to Japan. On 13 August,

Li Chuanhua, Deputy Director of the Propaganda Department of the CPC Central Committee stated: "The purpose of China's solemn commemoration of the 40th anniversary of the victory of the anti-Japanese war is to safeguard peace and to promote the Chinese to realise the reunification of the motherland and the Four modernizations with the strength of the great national unity and awakening the Chinese people achieved during the anti-Japanese War."

Secondly, on 15 August Yasuhiro Nakasone became the first postwar Japanese Prime Minister to make an official visit to the Yasukuni Shrine (that also contained the remains of Japan's condemned war criminals), ostensibly to honour the nations' war dead. The visit was loudly condemned in China. The veteran leader Peng Zhen, who had visited Japan only a few months earlier, was moved to describe the Yasukuni visit as "a mockery of the aspirations and sentiments of the Chinese and other Asian people."

Meanwhile Chinese leaders began to complain about the growing deficit that had developed in trade with Japan. Within the first 6 months of 1985 the deficit had reached $2.3 billion (exceeding the $2 billion total for the whole of 1984). The official news agency Xinhua, commenting on 1st August on the Ministerial meeting between Chinese State Counselor Gu Mu and Japanese Foreign Minister Shintaro Abe, pointed out that Japan had reduced imports of Chinese oil and silk and that it was sluggish in making investments in and transferring technology to China. From 1979 to 1984 Japan's $123 million accounted for only 9.2% of the total foreign investment in China. This was adjudged "incommensurate" with its share of one fourth of Chinese total foreign trade.[17]

On 18 September, offically approved demonstrations by students within their universities to mark the 56th anniversary of Japan's invasion of Manchuria spilled over into unauthorized demonstrations in the city centers against contemporary Japan. About one thousand students from Beijing University marched to Tiananmen Square shouting anti-Japanese slogans such as "Down with Nakasone," "Down with Japanese militarism," "strongly oppose the second invasion." A banner stated, "Let us never forget the national humiliation and continue to rely on our own strength"; another banner proclaimed: "I used to be a Japanese imperialist, decapitating 50 people in Shenyang, but now I'm selling you color TVs." The Chinese government was evidently embarrassed for the official media ignored all this and noted only the authorized parts of the demonstration.[18] Later, it transpired that similar demonstrations had taken place in at least three other cities. Two weeks later 3 days of violent anti-Japanese demonstrations that included some 50,000 students from 10 major colleges took place in Xian.[19]

These and other demonstrations sparked off extensive discussions in the official press on the nature of patriotism and the open door, the main point of which was to assert that the present position cannot be compared to the period before 1949 because, unlike the previous era the Chinese people now enjoy full sovereignty and they have full control over foreign economic relations. As the open door is crucial for the success of the modernization program that will bring prosperity and strength to China it is a patriotic duty to support it.[20] More to the point perhaps was the *China Daily* article of 15 October that flatly stated: "It is wrong for anyone to try to get rid of the Party's leadership or negate the policy of opening to the outside world under the pretext of democracy and legality."

Although China's leaders were able to take over the planned demonstrations of the 50th anniversary of the December 9th Movement (that in 1935 had helped to galvanize resistance to Japan in China's cities), student discontent and protest still simmered in many universities in the major cities, and it was thought that they were being encouraged if not manipulated by conservative elements in the higher reaches of the Party.[21] In the light of these developments, China's leaders, however, were able to extract some concessions from Japan. Thus Nakasone cancelled his second scheduled visit to the Yasukuni shrine in October, and Deng Xiaoping was able to tell visiting Foreign Minister Abe on 11 October that both Japan and China "should make efforts to avoid an incident or situation which would cause offense to the people[s of both countries.]"

These events not only cast a cloud on Sino-Japanese relations, but they proved highly embarrassing to China's leading reformers. No less a figure than Hu Yaobang had gone out of his way to give special emphasis to Sino-Japanese relations and on 18 October he found it necessary to add a further four points to the four he had already advanced as guidelines to the 21st Century Committee for Sino-Japanese Friendship.[22]

Another potentially greatly embarrassing issue in Sino-Japanese relations was the establishment of a Japanese Committee to honour the memory of Chiang Kai-Shek headed by former Prime Minister Kishi—the father-in-law of Foreign Minister Abe. So far this has only been publicized in the pro-Beijing Hong Kong press, but the issue could be explosive in the current climate in Beijing. Whether or not the conservatives associated with Chen Yun played a role in instigating the students there was no doubt that they benefited from the way the reformist leaders had been thrust on the defensive on issues concerning reform and the open door with even their patriotism impugned. It remains to be seen, however, what precise impact all this will have on Sino-Japanese relations. The relationship is too important to both sides for either set of leaders to allow it to be deflected by student demonstrations. But the episode illustrates how rapidly current complaints can be allied to historic grievances to unleash anti-foreign passions.

China and the Asia-Pacific Region

It is customary to regard China's policy in its region as largely an attribute of China's global policy orientations, particularly vis-à-vis the two superpowers, rather than as a series of bilateral relations with neighbors.[23] However, there were signs in 1985 of a more differentiated policy. Thus, despite China's emphasis on peace as part of its independent policy, China's policies towards Indochina have hardly changed since 1979. China has continued to wage a war of attrition and isolation on Vietnam. It has also forged a de facto alliance with Thailand by which China undertook to respond in the event of a Vietnamese attack on Thai territory during its customary dry season offensive.[24] China's leaders also ridiculed Vietnam's undertaking to withdraw its forces from Cambodia by 1990 that was announced at the meeting of the three Indochinese Foreign Ministers on August 15 and 16 in Phnom Penh, and they condemned other Vietnamese proposals as propaganda and lies.

China was able to make progress in cultivating the countries of ASEAN—including Indonesia and Malaysia whose governments have habitually been more sympathetic towards Vietnam and suspicious of China. In particular special efforts have been made to upgrade economic relations. These have been most highly developed with Singapore. Trade in 1984 exceeded $1.4 billion and was expected to reach $2 billion in 1985. Singaporean businessmen have invested over $80 million in China since 1983. In June 1985 Dr. Goh Keng Swee, the former Singapore Vice Premier, accepted appointment as an adviser on China's coastal economic development. As to be expected, economic and trade relations with Thailand were also regarded as satisfactory in China. In 1984 trade was valued at $330 million. Meanwhile, various agreements on joint projects and the promotion and protection of investments have been signed since 1980, including some important ones in 1985. Notwithstanding the problems of the Marcos regime and the Communist uprising in the Philippines, China continued to develop cordial and cooperative relations. Following the signing of a trade protocol in January, further agreements were signed on economic cooperation in March and July. Relations with Malaysia blossomed as Kuala Lumpur sought to improve economic relations and reduce restrictions on visits by its citizens to China. Prime Minister Mahathir bin Mohammed visited China with an economic delegation 130 strong and agreed on ways to augment trade and other economic relations. They also narrowed their differences on Vietnam. In July President Suharto of Indonesia finally authorized direct trade with China. Chinese and Indonesian trade delegations exchanged visits and signed letters of intent and trade contracts.[25]

Although China and the countries of ASEAN might be seen as long-term competitors for the same international markets, both sides took active measures to reduce the ways in which they might be trade rivals and to augment their economic relations in such a way as to extend their strategic accommodation on Vietnam to the economic spheres. This did not mean that their differences on Communist Parties in Southeast Asia, or on ethnic Chinese, or on Chinese claims to the island groups in the South China Seas, had been resolved. Rather it meant that some of their misapprehensions had been reduced and that the prospects for cooperative relations increased.

In a similar vein China's relations with the countries of South Asia also improved. The points of conflict were minimized. Border trade between Nepal and India on the one side and Tibet on the other expanded. Relations with Rajiv Gandhi's India were easier than with that of his mother even though the fundamental border issues remained unresolved. China welcomed the emergence in December of the South Asian Association for Regional Cooperation (SAARC) noting that without it the political problems between the countries of the area would have been even more destructive and that the agreement to establish SAARC may "generate needed momentum to battle the cross-currents and prompt brighter prospects for the region."[26]

China also intensified its good relations with Australia and New Zealand and used these as stepping stones to develop relations with the island countries of the South Pacific. Hu Yaobang visited Australia, New Zealand, Western Samoa, Fiji and Papua New Guinea in a 12 day tour in April. As we have seen, he gave approval to New Zealand's Labour Government's refusal to allow visits by U.S. naval nuclear ships. Still later China gave cautious approval to the declaration by the South Pacific Forum of a Nuclear Free Zone in the South Pacific. China's position was not entirely consistent, as China itself has used South Pacific waters as a target for its long range rockets. Moreover China has generally supported the French nuclear program (the main target of the South Pacific Forum) with which its own nuclear capacities have often been compared. Interestingly, China has yet formally to endorse the Declaration as all 5 nuclear powers were requested to do. The issue has acquired increased significance in view of the growing Soviet interest in this vast region, which hitherto has been within exclusively Western spheres of interest.

Much further to the north, on the Korean peninsula the impact of the superpowers was more apparent on China's foreign policy. And contrary to much of the rhetoric of the independent foreign policy it was clear that Sino-Soviet rivalry was complemented by a parallelism of Sino-American interests. To be sure, both themes were understated in public, but they were evident nonetheless. For some time North Korea had been pressing Moscow for the supply of advanced MIG 23s as a response to the F15s that President Reagan had decided to sell to the South. The Chinese attempted to cultivate the North and forestall the Soviet link by encouraging the North to seek a rapprochement with South and develop its troubled economy by following China's example of opening to the West. Deng Xiaoping and Hu Yaobang even went so far as to endorse the dynastic succesion by welcoming Kim Il Sung's son and heir apparent Kim Jong Il in June 1983. However, Kim acquired the Soviet aircraft after a Soviet agreement in November 1984, and he opened North Korean ports to visits by Soviet naval vessels, allowed the Soviet Union overflight rights, and gave permission to install intelligence and communications equipment in North Korea. This gave the Soviet Union a tangible presence in the North that is bound to increase the military pressure on China's Northeast (Manchuria). Nevertheless at the same time the North also reduced tension with the South, culminating in a highly symbolic exchange of 50 family visits in September. Yet observers felt that Moscow's influence had grown in Pyongyang. A graphic demonstration of this was the greater honour accorded the visiting Soviet delegation in August to mark the 40th anniversary of the Soviet liberation of the North as compared to that given the Chinese delegation in October to mark the 35th anniversary of the entry of Chinese forces into the Korean War.

Sino-Soviet competition in the North should not be thought of as a zero-sum game. Neither has an interest in the renewal of the Korean War and the North clearly perceives an interest in maintaining relations with both. Beijing, however, has an evident interest in promoting an accommodation between North and South that Moscow does not share. Moreover, Beijing is able to use its burgeoning but unofficial relations with the South as leverage against the North. The indirect trade between China and the South is thought to have reached $500 million in 1984. But China is also useful to the North in pressing the United States to hold talks with the North.[27] The situation is too sensitive for China to act openly as a host or an intermediary between the North on the one side and the United States (plus the South) on the other. China has pressed Washington to make concessions to the North for which China would hope to claim some credit. The United States, however, has its own commitments to the South. Thus although Washington and Beijing doubtless would prefer to see the division of Korea stabilized and Soviet influence minimized they are nevertheless constrained by their respective commitments to South and North from effective cooperation. Perhaps one visible key to North-South relations will be whether they can find mutually agreeable arrangements for the South's hosting of the Asian Games in 1986 and, more importantly, the Olympic Games in 1988.

As to be expected, following the agreement on Hong Kong Beijing intensified its campaign for reunification with Taiwan on a similar scheme of "one country two systems." Unofficial contacts have continued to take place such as indirect trade through Hong Kong and visits by people from Taiwan to the mainland. But no real movement has taken place on the issue. Moreover although Taiwan is the major irritant in Sino-American relations to be raised by China on the agenda in any high level talks between the two sides, Beijing seemed to be satisfied that the United States was observing the terms of the 1983 Communique in limiting its arms supplies to the island. As we have seen, the possible links between conservative LDP leaders in Japan and certain politicians in Taiwan could be a major source of concern in Beijing.

The significance of the Hong Kong question goes beyond the future of the territory itself. Any major instability or economic downturn would damage such prospects as exist for a peaceful reunification with Taiwan. China's international credibility would also be affected and that would threaten the success of the open door policies. Moreover the Hong Kong issue has the potential to affect for good or for ill the process of modernization in China and the politics of reform associated with it. Thus a great deal hangs not only on the way in which China would carry out the terms of the agreement with the British after 1997, but, more importantly, how it handles the intervening transitional period. The Chinese view is that sovereignty and administration of Hong Kong will be passed from Britain to China which will then administer the territory as a Special Administrative Region according to a Basic Law that will incorporate the detailed provisions of the 1984 agreement. The Basic Law will be enacted by the National People's Congress in Beijing in 1990. In the process the Chinese intend to consult with the people of Hong Kong. The British side has sought to expand the democratic base of representation in Hong Kong—a process that had started well before Sino-British negotiations began in 1982. Moreover certain professional and middle class groups began to press for a greater degree of democracy. Chinese unease with these developments eventually came to the surface when on 12 November Xu Jiatun, head of the local Xinhua News Agency office and hence the leading PRC representative on the territory accused the British of violating the spirit of the Sino-British agreement. Chinese officials then backed away from the extremity of the statement, but nevertheless they ensured that henceforth Beijing would be consulted prior to the development of further political reforms. Beijing has long since dropped its slogan of Gang Ren Zhi Gang (Hong Kong People will govern Hong Kong). Its principal concern is with the maintenance of stability and prosperity. Fortunately, from Beijing's perspective neither the Hong Kong currency nor stock exchange dropped substantially. But to judge from the non-leftist press, the interested professional and middle class groups were shaken by the experience.[28]

Europe and the Third World

The formulation of the independent foreign policy has involved an accentuation of China's relations with the European countries of East and West as well as with the countries of the Third World. Major efforts were made to cultivate relations and expand ties with the EEC and East European countries. High level visits took place between both sets of countries. A variety of agreements were signed with the East Europeans and the value of their trade was put at $2.5 billion. This had advantages for both sides as it did not involve precious hard currency. The ultimate constraint on these relations is the political quality of Sino-Soviet relations. Relations with both sides of the European divide were also an important part of the politics of China's foreign relations. It involved a Chinese attempt to support and further develop a softening of the old divisions in the hope that both sides would increase the pressure on their respective superpower allies to ameliorate international tension. It also was hoped to diversify China's economic relations. Trade with Western Europe was still deemed to fall short of its potential, counting at present for only about a third of the value of trade with Japan.

If China's foreign policy were to be judged primarily by its declaratory dimensions and the number and visibility of its diplomatic exchanges, the Third World would appear to be highly significant in the conduct of China's relations. In terms of the hard realities of strategic and economic concerns this is far from the case. But the Third World is nevertheless important in the relatively intangible dimensions of China's cultural self-image and its historical identity. By virtue of China having been a victim of imperialism and because of its struggle for economic development, China's leaders have long perceived it as an integral member of the Third World. One of the major appeals of the independent foreign policy is that it has enabled China's leaders to revive that dimension of China's foreign relations. This is also an area in which China's leaders have been able to criticize both superpowers with relative impunity. Perhaps the most practical aspect of its Third World relations in 1985 was Premier Zhao's visit to four countries in Latin America—the first ever such visit by a Chinese Prime Minister.

Conclusions

The developments of 1985 illustrated both the strengths and the weaknesses of China's much heralded independent foreign policy. Since 1982 China's leaders have registered useful gains by projecting their country's posture as relatively equidistant from the two superpowers. However, their reaction to the Geneva summit suggests that their freedom of maneuver was more dependent on the character of superpower relations than was previously apparent.

However, at the heart of China's policies (domestic and external) is the goal of modernization. The policies of the open door that are deemed essential for successful economic development have brought the external world into closer interactions with Chinese society. On the one hand this may be seen as an essential stimulus for reform, but on the other this has also exposed foreign relations to the unpredictable social/political upheavals that are an inevitable concomitant of the reforms. During the last quarter of 1985 Japan became the principal target for popular wrath—much to the embarrassment of the reformers Deng Xiaoping and Hu Yaobang. The significance of these developments, however, can be exaggerated since the consistent trend of the last six years has been for China to become increasingly engaged and interlocked with the international economy.

To return to the question posed at the outset it would seem that in the harsh realms of geopolitics China's foreign policy is less independent than its leaders proclaim. In practice China still leans to the American side, but it is seeking to balance that by better relations with the Russians. Similarly in foreign economic relations, China is seeking to supplement its increasingly interdependent economic ties with the Western world by deepening its ties with the Soviet world. As China has begun to embark on its seventh Five Year Plan, its leaders and their principal foreign policy advisors argue that their international environment will be relatively "tranquil" and that this will be conducive to the achievement of their domestic economic goals. If they are right, the main problems in foreign relations will be those involving the interactions between the external world and Chinese society.

Notes

The author is grateful to Dorothy J. Solinger and to an anonymous reader for their helpful suggestions in improving an earlier draft of this essay.

1. For accounts of the emergence of China's new foreign policy in the 1980s see Carol Lee Hamrin, "China Reassesses the Superpowers," *Pacific Affairs* Summer, 1983, pp. 209–231; Harry Harding, "China's Changing Role in the Contemporary World," in Harry Harding, ed., *China's Foreign Relations in the 1980s* (New Haven: Yale University Press, 1984) pp. 177–223; and Steven M. Goldstein, "Foreign Policy," in Steven M. Goldstein, ed., *China Briefing 1984* (Boulder, CO: Westview Press, 1985) pp. 61–62.

2. See Mary Lee, "Winter of Discontent," *Far Eastern Economic Review (FEER)*, 5 December 1985, p. 16, and *Cheng Ming* 99 in *Foreign Broadcast Information Service Daily Report, China (FBIS)*, 6 January 1986, W1–6.

3. Deng Xiaoping, *Build Socialism with Chinese Characteristics* (Beijing: Foreign Languages Press, 1985), p. 29.

4. Goldstein, *op. cit.*, p. 68.

5. *Beijing Review (BR)*, January 7, 1985, p. 6.

6. Hong Kong, *Hsin Wan Pao*, 9 April, in *FBIS*, 9 April 1985, W2.

7. *BR*, July 19, 1985, p. 6.

8. *New York Times*, January 6, 1986, p. 20. There is confusion in Chinese official figures as two government agencies have released conflicting figures. See *FEER*, February 6, 1986, p. 55 and March 20, 1986, pp. 91–93.

9. *FBIS*, 2 August 1985, D2.

10. For a detailed survey of these see Xiao Yongzhan, "Sino-U.S. Trade Ties and Legal Exchanges," in *BR*, July 8, 1985, pp. 20–22.

11. *FBIS*, 8 November 1985, C1.

12. The above two paragraphs drew on Richard Nations, "Point Counterpoint," *FEER*, 12 December 1985, p. 16 and John F. Burns, "China Rejects a Nonaggression Pact with Soviet," *New York Times*, 16 January 1986.

13. See Richard Nations, *loc. cit.*

14. "Qian Qichan Reviews China's Foreign Policy," in *BR*, January 6, 1986, p. 15.

15. *BR*, May 6, 1985, p. 8.

16. For further discussion see Allen S. Whiting, "Assertive Nationalism in Chinese Foreign Policy," *Asian Survey*, Vol. 23, No. 8, August 1983.

17. *FBIS*, 2 August 1985, D2. See also Charles Smith, "Chinese Buy—Japanese Binge Strains the Relationship," *FEER*, 1 August 1985, pp. 46–47.

18. *FBIS*, 19 September 1985, D1.

19. See for example, *Chinese Youth Paper (Zhongguo Qingnian Bao)* 26 October 1985, p. 1 ff in *FBIS*, 12 November 1985, K8-K12.

20. *China Daily*, 7 November 1985, p. 3 and *Cheng Ming* (Hong Kong) 16 November, pp. 3–7, in *FBIS*, 18 November 1985, W1-W6.

21. *BR*, October 28, 1985, p. 6.

22. See for example, *BR*, October 28, 1985, p. 6.

23. A *People's Daily* article of 4 November outlined in some detail Vietnam's economic difficulties and argued that these would not be resolved as long as Vietnam's rulers persisted in "aggression and expansion." *FBIS*, 12 November 1985, E2-E3.

24. *FBIS*, 21 November 1985, E1-E7.

25. *BR*, December 16, 1985, pp. 11–12.

26. The above account has drawn heavily from Richard Nations, "China's Korea Fiasco" *FEER*, 26 September 1985, p. 56 and Nayan Chanda, "Pyongyang Revisited" *FEER*, 7 November 1985, pp. 18–19.

27. *FBIS*, 18 October 1985, W3-W6.

28. For detailed accounts see the articles by Emily Lau in *FEER*, 19 September, 12 December, 26 December 1985 and 2 January 1986.

3
Social Ferment: Grumbling Amidst Growth

Elizabeth J. Perry

China's post-Mao reforms have received considerable international applause recently. Just as Maoism was once heralded as an alternative route to modernity—distinct from industrialization of either the western or the Soviet type—so today Deng Xiaoping's unique brand of "market socialism" is already being hailed by outside observers as a welcome new development strategy for Third World nations.

Time Magazine, which chose Deng Xiaoping as its Man of the Year for 1985, speculated on the momentous consequences of successful Chinese modernization under Deng's innovative leadership:

> Communists everywhere, notably in the Third World, would see an alternative to the failure of Soviet-style Marxism. Many of China's neighbors in the Far East, including Taiwan and South Korea, would find that a political foe had been tamed into a trading partner, while an economic weakling had become a mighty competitor. Most important, perhaps, the U.S. and other Western countries would see the crusading faith that has made the Marxist third of the world an enemy converted into a system that the West could live with and in some respects, though certainly not all, applaud.[1]

It is true that under Deng's new policies the Chinese economy—particularly the agricultural sector—has shown impressive growth over the past six years. The return to family farming (with the introduction of household responsibility systems which de-collectivized agricultural production) was accompanied by price reform, relaxation of state procurement quotas, and liberalization of cropping, sideline production and marketing. This reform package showed almost immediate—and dramatic—results. Yields of key cash crops, such as cotton and oil, shot up by annual rates of 15 to 20 percent, while grain output also evidenced a steady increase. Average peasant incomes soared by more than 10 percent per year, in contrast to the previous two decades of stagnation. The first signs of a retrenchment in this almost miraculous record of agricultural achievement became visible only in 1985, with a drop in grain production of some 6 percent over the previous year. But even with this sharp downturn, the 1985 harvest was reportedly still the third largest in Chinese history. Granaries remain full from bumper crops of the past three years.

Reforms in the industrial sector, although initially less radical than the new rural policies, also spelled change. A new system of enterprise taxes, by which factories assumed greater responsibility for profits and losses, was implemented. Liberalization of material allocations, production plans, and marketing further increased the autonomy of individual enterprises. Still, industrial growth rates were sluggish when compared to the accomplishments of peasants in the countryside.[2]

In response to this imbalance, the year 1985 saw a change of focus in the thoroughgoing reforms that have swept post-Mao China. With results to date looking far more impressive in the rural areas than in the cities, the leaders decided at a Central Committee meeting in October 1984 to stress urban reform in the upcoming year.[3] Increased latitude for individual factories, encouragement of small private enterprises, promotion of intermediate towns, and reduced state responsibility for urban planning and welfare marked the change in emphasis.

Regardless of how successful these new policies may prove in enhancing industrial performance—and the chapter by Barry Naughton cautions against undue optimism here—it is already clear that the urban reforms, like the rural reforms which preceded them, are generating a good deal of social ferment. This is hardly surprising. Programs which fundamentally restructure the processes of production and control are bound to elicit spirited reactions from those whose lives have been radically altered. That the post-Mao reforms have given rise to social unrest is probably more a testimony to the thoroughgoing character of these policies than an omen of their demise. Even so, an examination of such social tensions allows us to assess the obstacles to Deng Xiaoping's reform effort and facilitates an evaluation of the costs and benefits of the endeavor.

The implementation of household responsibility systems among the peasantry was followed in the early 1980's by a flood of press reports about rural unrest. Often mobilized by disgruntled cadres (whose powers had been undermined by decollectivization), peasants were pictured as engaging in greedy attacks on the property of state and fellow peasants alike. Tales of feuds and looting sprees—sometimes buttressed by religious rituals—appeared frequently. The subsequent program to "let some peasants get rich first," a policy intended to encourage rural commercialization, has further fanned the flames of rural discontent. Jealousy towards newly rich peasants (some of whom enjoy incomes one hundred times that of their less fortunate neighbors) is blamed for a good deal of hostility and violence.

For the most part, these instances of rural unrest seem to have been small in scale and directed against parochial targets rather than against government policies per se. Increased inequality among peasants in some areas has generated real resentment, but there is little indication that serious animosities are extended to the reform program as a whole. Much enriched, on average, by the new policies, most peasants appear content to limit any grumbling to local competitors, rather than call into question programs which have been demonstrably successful in filling both government granaries and peasant purses.[4]

Just as rural unrest accompanied the implementation of agricultural reforms, so the recent shift toward urban reform has given rise to a number of city-centered problems. Lurid revelations of economic crime and corruption captured headlines early in 1985, while concerns about student protest developed over the fall and winter months. Compared to the situation in the countryside, urban unrest as it unfolded over the past year threatened to pose some serious political challenges. Reform-minded leaders are the first to point out that the resolution of such problems is essential if they are to achieve their stated goal of building "a socialist country with Chinese characteristics."

Urban Protest

The government's effort to reduce some of its enormous expenditures on urban subsidies (which amount to about one-quarter of total state revenues) prompted a speedy and hostile student response early in the year. In January, students at Beijing Normal University launched a successful wall-poster campaign (an unconstitutional method of protest in post-Mao China) opposing a Ministry of Education directive which would have eliminated student stipends during winter and spring breaks.

Three months later, Beijing saw further protest when several hundred sent-down youths returned to the capital to stage a sit-down demonstration. Having left Beijing in 1968 to work in the remote countryside as part of the Maoist "down to the villages, up to the mountains" movement, these displaced individuals now demanded repatriation to their homes. Despite a vociferous show of strength in front of the Beijing municipal party committee office, the youths were asked to return to the countryside without any redress of grievances.[5]

In May, Beijing was again rocked with youthful unrest. Defeat of China's soccer team by Hong Kong led to a post-game riot outside the stadium. More than 100 people—mostly between the ages of 17 and 25—were arrested for their part in the disturbance, which involved attacks on foreigners and foreign cars. In the end, however, only three of the participating youths were punished for the incident—with jail sentences of six to thirty months.

This background of unrest, and its rather lenient treatment by the authorities, helped set the stage for the more serious student protests which erupted across Chinese campuses in the fall. On September 12, students at Beijing University put up a big-character poster calling for a September 18 march on Tiananmen Square. Coming only a few weeks after Japanese Prime Minister Nakasone's controversial visit to the Yasukuni Shrine war memorial, the march—scheduled for the anniversary of the 1931 Manchurian incident—was ostensibly intended to commemorate Chinese who had died in fighting the Japanese during World War II, to oppose a revival of Japanese militarism, and to resist a contemporary Japanese economic invasion of China. The spirit of protest quickly spread to other campuses in Beijing and Xian, with big-character posters calling upon students to join the September 18 demonstration and to boycott Japanese goods.

It is easy enough to find reasons for the students' anti-Japanese sentiments: China's trade deficit with Japan was expected to run to U.S. $5 billion in 1985 and the Chinese government itself had stirred popular emotions by forcefully protesting the revival of Japanese militarism at the time of Nakasone's Yasukuni Shrine visit. Nevertheless, the student unrest received a less than enthusiastic reception from Chinese leaders. Having recently witnessed anti-foreign violence in the Beijing soccer riots, authorities must have feared that a large-scale student demonstration could easily deteriorate into another xenophobic display. Even more upsetting, however, was the fact that the students were not limiting their grievances to the Japanese. The charge of Japanese economic invasion was of course an implicit criticism of the Chinese government's open door foreign policy, but some student posters went further in complaints about high commodity prices and requests for more freedom and democracy at home. Carrying banners which read "We want to eat," demonstrators bemoaned the inflation and cadre corruption that had followed in the wake of recent price reforms.

In an attempt to dampen the fires of campus unrest, universities were put under strict surveillance and students were enjoined to cancel the September 18 march. Despite this strong government response, a number of students managed to sneak out of their campuses and carry floral wreaths to the Monument of People's Heroes on the appointed day. Moreover, leaders of the march called for further protests on yet another anti-Japanese anniversary: December 9, a date when, fifty years before, students in Beijing had voiced vehement opposition toward Japanese aggression.

As preparations for the December 9th anniversary developed, student activists publicized slogans calling for opposition to bureaucratism and "unhealthy tendencies" and repudiation of people who seek wealth and power by betraying their country. Such slogans, which resonated with themes in veteran economic planner Chen Yun's critical speech delivered at the National Party Conference in September, gave rise to suspicions that the students may have enjoyed backing from high-level leaders dissatisfied with the direction and pace of some of Deng Xiaoping's reforms. Blaming the fall in grain production on reduced central control, Chen warned in September that "grain shortages will lead to social disorder."[6] Rumors circulated that the protesters—most of whom were reportedly graduate students at Beijing and Qinghua universities—included sons and daughters of the 131 high-ranking Party veterans who had fallen from power at the September party conference. The alleged links between student dissidents and disgruntled cadres may have raised the spectre of Red Guard activities during the Cultural Revolution. In any case, the authorities reacted to the December 9th preparations with extraordinary concern. Vice-Premier Li Peng, director of the new National Education Commission which replaced the dismantled Ministry of Education, played a prominent role in meeting with students and calming campus tensions. Thanks apparently to the adroit negotiations of this "adopted son" of the late Premier Zhou Enlai, massive student demonstrations were averted in favor of participation in state-sponsored anniversary events.[7]

Successful handling of the December 9th activities did not insulate the state from further protest, however. That same month hundreds of minority students from Xinjiang province staged a demonstration in Beijing calling for an end to nuclear testing in their homeland. The students, carrying banners, marched on Tiananmen Square and then gathered in front of Zhongnanhai to deliver a petition which called for a halt to nuclear tests, democratic election of minorities to replace Han Chinese officials, an end to coercive family planning among minorities, increased support for minority education, economic self-determination, support for the anti-nuclear movement in Xinjiang (where a one-day protest on December 12 had involved thousands of students), and an end to the practice of banishing convicted Chinese criminals to their homeland. A few days later, about a hundred Uighur students in Shanghai marched through the center of the city with banners which read "Stop nuclear tests" and "Don't turn Xinjiang into a concentration camp."[8]

Although student demonstrations do not seem to have resulted in any major shifts in government policy, at least one of the students' complaints—of "unhealthy tendencies" among officials—has become a dominant theme of Party rectification work in recent months.

"Unhealthy Tendencies"

In light of the heady new opportunities for profit-making which China's economic reforms have suddenly opened up, it is hardly surprising that entrepreneurial instincts should sometimes get the better of bureaucrats. This is particularly true inasmuch as official guidelines for proper economic behavior have been rather hazy. Moreover, at a time when the Party has opened wide its doors to newly rich peasants and other financial beneficiaries of the reforms, it is perhaps only natural that cadres too should be attracted by the Party-sponsored slogan that "to get rich is glorious." Unfortunately, however, a substantial number of cadres pursued paths to riches which were soon denounced as "unhealthy" by popular tabloids and Party discipline inspection commissions alike.

The most notorious of these incidents to come to light in 1985 was the Hainan scandal. This sensational deal involved massive buying of foreign exchange and importation from Hong Kong of U.S. $1.5 billion worth of goods—ranging from Mercedes limousines to color television sets—for resale at high rates of profit. Prominent officials in Party, government and military were implicated in the venture. But the Hainan was just one of hundreds of such startling incidents to be reported in the Chinese press last year. In Heilongjiang province, for example, a branch of the Harbin public security bureau set up a bogus firm which resold steel products at huge profits. In the special economic zone of Shenzhen, a member of the municipal Party committee and director of the municipal commission on politics and law was arrested for engaging in speculation and encouraging smuggling activities.[9]

Demobilized soldiers provided an important source of economic criminals. According to a June announcement by Deng Xiaoping, who continues to chair the General Military Commission, the People's Liberation Army was to be cut by one million men in 1985–86, with half of the cuts coming from the officer corps. Suddenly faced with unemployment, more than a few of these former military personnel turned to illegal economic ventures. *People's Daily* publicized the case of one such demobilized officer who set up a fake trading company and signed nineteen contracts to import some 200,000 non-existent television sets. The former soldier secured an advance payment of more than 12.6 billion yuan from over 100 units in ten provinces before his arrest.

On-duty officials were, however, an even more troubling source of economic criminals. In September, Chen Yun reported disapprovingly that during the past year alone, Party and government cadres or their children had started 20,000 private businesses, many of which were in cahoots with lawbreakers—both Chinese and foreign. Furthermore, about half of the managers of state enterprises were believed to cheat on their corporate income taxes. To combat such "unhealthy tendencies," central and provincial state and Party units issued a steady stream of circulars and prohibitions. Officials were explicitly warned against a whole menu of abuses: Engaging in trade or running enterprises on their own or in the names of their friends or relatives; arbitrarily raising prices; reselling for profit imported goods in short supply; reselling foreign exchange for profit; spending production funds as consumption funds for subsidies and rewards; favoritism in issuing lottery or raffle tickets; squandering public funds for extravagant feasting, drinking, travel, and gift-giving; indiscriminately sending personnel abroad; bribery, embezzlement, and the like.

Correcting such malpractices was a central focus of the second stage of Party rectification undertaken by many units in 1985. Cadres charged with "unhealthy tendencies" were to be denied re-registration. On the other hand, Party membership was to be warmly extended to groups whose support is considered essential for the success of China's ambitious modernization program—especially intellectuals and individuals who have prospered under the reforms. In the cities, admission of college students was emphasized. A springtime Party recruitment drive in the city of Shanghai, for example resulted in the admission of many new members, 67 percent of whom were intellectuals (with educational levels of technical secondary school or above). In the intermediate towns, private enterprise workers were welcomed. As a Party report noted, ". . . there are many private enterprise workers who are becoming richer and richer day by day and they wholeheartedly love socialism. The door of the Party is wide open to all private enterprise workers who have met Party membership qualifications." In the countryside, newly rich peasants were a principal recruitment target.[10]

Newly Rich Peasants

The newly rich peasants, lauded in the national press as harbingers of general rural prosperity, are rather controversial figures in their own local areas. Drawn largely from the ranks of former cadres, demobilized soldiers, returned educated youths, skilled artisans and experienced entrepreneurs, the newly commercialized peasants constitute a potentially unsettling force in the countryside. Although wooed in Party recruitment drives, these parvenues are sometimes resented by fellow peasants—and, more importantly, by rural cadres—who have done less well under the recent reforms. As the Chinese press noted, "Some people, having gotten used to 'eating from the common pot' in the past, resort. . . not to the path of getting rich by diligence, but instead feel a rage of envy. Among such people there are common plebians but most of them are also local potentates."[11]

If local cadres and peasants sometimes turn a cold shoulder to their *nouveaux riches* neighbors, such insults are usually more than outweighed by the government's red carpet treatment. Seen by the state as a vehicle for combatting lingering leftist tendencies, newly rich peasants are rewarded by government authorities with everything from sewing machines to Party membership. In the short run, they provide what is seen by state leaders as healthy competition to recalcitrant rural cadres. In the longer run, however, one cannot help but wonder whether they will not also come to pose a serious challenge to state control. Peasant entrepreneurs—whose shops offer a wider choice of goods at lower prices—threaten the once monopolistic powers of state-operated supply and marketing cooperatives and grain stations. For the first time in decades, state economic units face genuine competition from independent peasant businesses. As rich peasants gain increased economic and political clout, they may soon be in a position to promote their own interests in a manner that challenges state, as well as collective, control.

With the state and collectives withdrawing from some of their traditional responsibilities in the countryside, newly rich peasants are expected to step in to fill the gap. Stories describing the charitable deeds of peasant entrepreneurs were frequent in 1985. Now that fewer resources are available to teams and villages under the household responsibility system, those individuals who have prospered under the system are called upon to contribute from their personal wealth to various local projects. Like the gentry of pre-liberation days, the well-off today are once again expected to construct schools, roads, and water works; provide ready low-interest loans to neighbors in need; and underwrite community activities. Such benevolence probably reflects not only Party pressure, but also the personal desire of many newly rich peasants to defuse local jealousies. Although per capita peasant incomes have soared in recent years, the wealth has not been evenly distributed. As long as there are glaring income disparities among villagers—and Deng Xiaoping declared in January 1985 that "there are still some tens of millions of peasants who do not have enough food"—we may expect to see continuing resentment against the rural rich.

Urbanization

In the long run, the Chinese government hopes to combat the problem of rural poverty through the development of intermediate towns (*xiao chengzhen*)—centers of rural industry and commerce which will absorb the surplus labor of the countryside. Currently peasants are being encouraged to move to these towns to start factories and shops. Newly rich peasants, in particular, are enjoined to invest some of their wealth (and their children's labor) in new private enterprises. By the year 2000, China expects that some 30 percent of the rural population will have resettled in these intermediate towns.[12]

In encouraging peasants to move into more urbanized settlements, the Chinese regime is making a momentous break with the policy of the past thirty years. Since 1958, strict migration controls have prevented peasants from leaving their native places. To avoid the problems of urban squalor so common among developing countries and to facilitate the tight controls believed necessary for socialist planning, migration from the countryside to the city was made all but impossible. Today, however, greater labor mobility is seen by the reformers as a necessary part of economic growth.

Peasant migrants help to fill the ranks of the private enterprise workers (*geti hu*) whose activities have contributed so much to the dynamism of the economy. At the same time, however, the movement of such large numbers of people has naturally created certain difficulties for social control. Much attention is now being given to the problem of the "floating population"—persons who reside in the cities, yet retain rural household registrations. In many cities, the floating population is said to number some ten to twenty percent of the total population (in both Shanghai and Beijing, for example, the floating population is estimated at well over one million).[13] These new urbanites put a severe strain on public services which are in very short supply. The housing crunch has already reached desperate proportions. Although municipal authorities continue to return ownership rights to private homes confiscated during the Cultural Revolution, demand for decent dwellings far exceeds supply.

Food price increases are perhaps the principal complaint of Chinese urbanites. In 1985, compulsory state grain purchases were phased out (so as to alleviate the state's burden of costly subsidies) and the prices of pork, beef and dairy products were permitted to float in major urban markets. In most cities, state subsidies for food were seen by local residents as insufficient to keep pace with the price hikes. Unwelcome migrants from the countryside only intensified the grumbling of urban consumers.

Population Control

The burgeoning floating population in Chinese towns and cities also constitutes a potential source of deviance from family planning regulations. The difficulties of population control have already resulted in some relaxation of the stringent single-child family policy. Although China clings to its goal of keeping the population under 1.2 billion by the end of the century, the regime is now acknowledging that at least ten percent of rural couples should be permitted to have a second child "if necessary." In Guangdong province, families are being allowed to have a second child if their first-born is a daughter. In Shanxi province, considerable success has been claimed for a rural experiment in "late marriage, late child-bearing, plus an interval." According to this program, a woman who has her first child soon after marriage at age 23 or so may have a second child after waiting for an interval of over six years. The widespread adoption of this method, it is believed, would keep the population under 1.2 billion by the year 2000. Thus an accommodation with peasant demands for more children—demands which have only intensified with the return to family farming in recent years—seems on the horizon.[14]

Peasant desires for many offspring are reinforced by evidence that newly rich peasants tend to come from larger families. Households with enough labor power to farm their sizable responsibility lands as well as to branch out into more commercialized endeavors are most likely to have prospered under the recent agricultural reforms. In the model county of Fengyang (in Anhui province), for example, the richest peasant—Chen Xinghan—heads a ten-person family (augmented by an equal number of hired hands). Having just built an enormous house (complete with detached garden) at an expense of over 100,000 yuan, Chen is adamant that his eight offspring continue to live at home for as long as he remains alive. In a manner reminiscent of pre-liberation gentry, Chen abhors the prospect of family division. A large, united family is seen as synonymous with good fortune. The second most affluent peasant in Fengyang heads an 18-person family. Husband, wife, children, grandchildren, and in-laws each take responsibility for different economic pursuits.[15]

Households in the stage of the family cycle when producers outnumber consumers are particularly well situated to take advantage of opportunities created by the recent reforms. By allocating land on the basis of family size, the responsibility system creates many of the conditions once identified by A.V. Chayanov as the classic peasant economy. As Chayanov once noted, under such conditions demography comes to play a decisive role in the relative fortunes of different peasant households.[16] Age-old economic and cultural factors predispose Chinese peasants to prefer many children, especially sons. The introduction of household contracting only intensifies this traditional preference.

Education

Population control is not the only national policy to be altered by the household responsibility system. Rural education (as the chapter by Peter Seybolt explains in detail) is also in the midst of major change. With peasant families now permitted to retain as their own profit any production above the quota stipulated in their annual contract, it is difficult for villages to accumulate enough funds to run high quality schools. The tuition fees being charged in many areas are a serious burden to poor families. Furthermore, now that farming is done by individual households rather than collectively, many families find it preferable to keep children at home to help out with the chores rather than send them off for costly education. Although state policy is to encourage lengthier schooling for its citizens, the need for increased family labor has prompted more than a few parents to take their children out of the classroom.

The state has been unwilling to increase its budgeted allocation for education in the countryside, although a State Council directive has authorized local governments to devise their own surtaxes to raise funds for rural schools. Some provinces have responded to this central directive by encouraging relatively prosperous villages and townships to levy education surcharges—amounting to about one percent of local per capita income—on agriculture, rural industry, and commercial enterprises within their jurisdictions. Although the decision to exempt impoverished areas from such surtaxes is understandable, the result is certain to be a serious and growing gap in the quality of education between rich and poor locales.[17]

It is toward urban education that the newly constituted National Education Commission has devoted most of its attention. Higher education, in particular, is being expanded. Secondary-level vocational schools are now taking in well over 30 percent of the country's senior middle school students (up from only seven percent in 1978). Graduate student enrollments in 1985 were also up—60 percent above the previous year.[18]

Educational institutions and job units (rather than the state) are enjoying increased freedom in placing university and vocational school graduates. Such flexibility probably promotes job satisfaction on the part of both employer and employee, but it also generates inequities in hiring. Women graduates, for example, are finding it extremely difficult to secure positions commensurate with their educational attainments. An investigation by the Henan provincial Party committee revealed that over the past two years 70–80 percent of units in need of college graduates had selected only males; many of the units had explicitly refused to consider hiring a woman. The investigation found that many women had discontinued their studies, convinced of the futility of completing an academic degree.[19]

Centrifugal Tendencies

The picture for urban women was not without its bright spots, however. Large numbers of women—mostly middle-aged and elderly intellectuals—were admitted to the Communist Party in 1985. And women made a powerful showing in the courtroom, as well. Divorce cases have mushroomed in recent years, with women acting as plaintiffs in more than 70 percent of the cases last year. (It might also be noted, however, that more and more women have appeared in Chinese courtrooms under involuntary circumstances, as well. The number of female criminals has risen dramatically of late, with many of the culprits involved in gang activities, drug trafficking, and other serious felonies.)[20]

In keeping with trends of the past few years, the legal profession is playing an increased role in policy interpretation and enforcement. (The influence of legal opinion is indicated by the high subscription figures for popular legal magazines. The Beijing periodical, *Chinese Legal System*, enjoys a subscription level of 1.41 million readers; its Shanghai counterpart, *Democracy and Law*, boasted 2.6 million subscribers last year.) With only 18,000 lawyers in China—augmented annually by about 2,000 new law school graduates—the demand for legal advice far outstrips the available supply.[21] The enactment of a host of new laws (a marriage law, contract law, civil and criminal codes, etc.) in the post-Mao era has notably enhanced the importance of the legal arena. Whether the judiciary will become a force strong enough to act as a truly meaningful check on Party and state power is doubtful. Still, the growth of legal prerogative—even if intended to serve only reformist ends—is another indication of the centrifugal forces unleashed by Deng's market experiments.

These efferent tendencies have obviously injected a new dynamism into Chinese society. In the countryside, the material effects of the agricultural reforms are readily visible. The frantic pace of new housing construction and evidence of rampant consumerism in the form of new watches, bicycles, sewing machines, stereos—and even washing machines, refrigerators, and color televisions, is apparent to any casual observer. In the cities, small eateries (*xiao chi*) mushroomed along main streets and back alleys in 1985, encouraged in part by a State Council directive to reduce the official noon break to one hour (thus affording less time to return home for lunch). Recreational facilities flourished as well; in the city of Wuhan alone, some 30 dance halls opened last year.

Centrifugal developments add color and excitement to a once drab social existence, but they also create real concerns for Party leaders. Greater diversity among ordinary people endangers the control of those at the top of the political system.

Conclusions

Although largely economic in nature, the post-Mao reforms have engendered momentous social change. The growing pains recently experienced in both the cities and the countryside attest to the unsettling effects of Deng Xiaoping's ambitious modernization drive. It must be emphasized, however, that social tensions do not demonstrate the failure of the reform effort. They suggest, rather, that economic liberalization entails certain trade-offs.

China, like virtually every developing country, seeks to pursue at least three objectives simultaneously: economic growth, social equality, and political control. Growth entails an increase in gross national product; equality implies a fair distribution of the new wealth; and control refers to the government's capacity to maintain order in the face of rapid change. In the long run, these goals are probably mutually reinforcing: increased production should enhance the state's ability to redistribute resources and promote public order. In the short run, however, the goals are often contradictory, calling for difficult policy choices. Whereas previous Chinese leaders have placed priority upon equality (in the case of Mao Zedong) or control (in the case of Liu Shaoqi), Deng Xiaoping and his reformist colleagues have opted for economic growth as their primary objective.[22]

So long as China succeeds in maintaining impressive growth rates, the leadership can be expected to weather criticism from advocates of either a more egalitarian or a more bureaucratic bent. In 1985 this was still the situation. Neither student protesters nor high-placed critics were able to upset the momentum of market reform. If the economy should evidence a very marked deterioration, however, the grumbling of recent months could become political dynamite. De-collectivization, peasant enrichment programs, inflation, and reduced subsidies and services—developments which threaten both political control and social equality—

may be just the sorts of visible irritants to draw critics of different ideological persuasion together in opposition.

It is too early to predict with confidence the outcome of the historic reform effort in which China is now engaged. Undeniably, the past several years have seen dramatic economic growth coupled with some disturbing social problems. At present, the Chinese leadership judges the cost a necessary and affordable price for rapid modernization. Whether such a judgement can be sustained will determine the contours of Chinese society in the years ahead.

Notes

1. *Time Magazine*, January 6, 1986, p. 26.

2. For assessments of the relative success of reforms in agriculture and industry, see Elizabeth J. Perry and Christine Wong (eds.) *The Political Economy of Reform in Post-Mao China* (Cambridge, Ma.: Harvard University Press, 1985).

3. *Beijing Review*, October 29, 1984.

4. See Elizabeth J. Perry, "Rural Collective Violence in Socialist China" in *China Quarterly* (September 1985).

5. *Joint Publications Research Service* [hereafter JPRS] CPS, May 23, 1985, p. 31; *Foreign Broadcast Information Service, Daily Report, China* [hereafter FBIS], April 30, 1985, K1–2.

6. See Chen's speeches in *Beijing Review*, September 30, 1985 and October 14, 1985.

7. FBIS, November 18, 1985, W1; December 2, 1985, K6; December 9, 1985, K2.

8. *Zhong Bao*, Hong Kong, December 28, 1985.

9. JPRS - CPS, March 26, 1985, pp. 53–54.

10. JPRS - CPS, May 28, 1985, p. 79; July 31, 1985, p. 11.

11. JPRS - CPS, June 14, 1985, p. 85.

12. JPRS - CPS, March 26, 1985, p. 35.

13. FBIS, June 27, 1985, p. K1.

14. JPRS - CPS, April 16, 1985, p. 23; FBIS, November 20, 1985, W3.

15. Interview in Fengyang county.

16. A.V. Chayanov, *The Theory of Peasant Economy* (Homewood, Ill.: R.D. Irwin for The American Economic Association, 1966).

17. JPRS - CPS, March 13, 1985, p. 45; FBIS, April 16, O1.

18. JPRS - CPS, March 13, 1985, p. 43; April 1, 1985, p. 61.

19. FBIS, December 6, 1985, P3–4.

20. JPRS - CPS, April 15, 1985, p. 101.

21. JPRS - CPS, April 1, 1985, p. 63–64.

22. For an interpretation of Chinese politics as a struggle among three alternative approaches to socialist development (Maoist, bureaucratic and market), see Dorothy Solinger (ed.) *Three Visions of Chinese Socialism* (Boulder, Co.: Westview Press, 1984).

4
Economy

Barry J. Naughton

The Chinese economy was on a roller coaster ride for much of 1985. A dizzying surge of industrial growth that began at the end of 1984 accelerated through the first half of 1985, and attracted worldwide attention. Spectacular growth seemed to signal a new phase of China's economic development: During the first half of the year industrial output was 24% above the same period in 1984, and industry expanded by 18% in all of 1985.[1] Yet, by midyear, it became obvious that this growth spurt had created serious tensions in the economy, and urgent measures to reduce the growth rate of industrial production and investment were adopted. Moreover, hit by bad weather and a shift in acreage away from grain production, China's total grain output plunged from the record harvest of 1984. By the end of the year, planners had brought growth rates down to a sustainable level, and ample grain stocks ruled out any danger of shortages of food grain. Nevertheless, a mood of uncertainty lingered, as planners contemplated their next moves. In particular, after a year in which economic reform measures had dominated policymaking, the need to restore macroeconomic balance seemed to rule out further progress in reform, at least in the immediate future.

The dramatic events of 1985 had their roots in the final quarter of 1984. Since 1979, the most innovative—and most successful—economic policies have been those carried out in the countryside. The excellent 1984 harvest seemed to demonstrate definitively the success of rural economic reforms, and emboldened China's leadership to enact a major program of economic reform in urban areas. A central committee document of October 1984 served as the charter for a series of sweeping reform initiatives, and dramatic changes took place in the urban economy in 1985. However, since these changes were in a sense predicated on previous rural changes, and since agriculture remains the primary activity of the large majority of the Chinese population, it makes sense to look at agriculture first.

Agriculture

The 1984 harvest was arguably the best harvest in the history of the People's Republic. Aided by exceptional weather, and the stabilization of market-oriented reforms, agricultural output increased by 11.7% (not including rural industrial production). Even more striking, grain production increased by 5.2%, notwithstanding a 1% decline in acreage, and surpassed the level of 400 million metric tons for the first time. (Ironically, this was the original 1985 target in the grandiose Ten Year Plan advanced under Hua Guofeng.) Cotton output increased by a remarkable 35%. Coming on the heels of two successive record harvests, these results seemed to indicate that China had finally emerged from an era in which overall economic progress was held back by slow growth of the agricultural sector. Most satisfying was the fact that improvements in efficiency traceable to rural reforms allowed a rapid expansion in the output of economic crops without sacrificing grain output.

The major impact of the 1984 harvest was, of course, highly favorable; however, the success had several secondary effects that called for careful economic policy making. First, the large harvest naturally created an even larger increase in peasant money income. The rapid growth in peasant purchasing power called for immediate measures to supply consumer goods to rural areas, and careful control of the overall balance between income and supply of consumer goods. Second, the apparent abundance led planners to reduce state control over grain marketing and lower the marginal purchase price of grain. During 1985, planners moved away from a system of compulsory procurement of grain and towards a system of contractual purchases, in which a single contract price replaced the former dual price (quota and above-quota) system. Since 1979, the state had been paying farmers a low price for compulsory grain deliveries, but a substantially higher price for all deliveries above the compulsory quota. The "above quota" price was substantially above the urban sale price for grain, and also above the price at which the government sells grain in the countryside. As a result, the state has been spending large sums to subsidize the transport and sale of grain in both rural and urban areas. Following a procedure first adopted in 1984 with respect to cotton, the government in 1985 initiated a new unitary price for grain. The new purchase price—which also became the rural sales price—was formed by taking 30% of the old quota price and 70% of the above-quota price: thus all grain would now be valued at a price between the two previous prices. (The urban sales price did not change.) It was expected that the unification of the rural purchase and sales price would lead to a reduction in government subsidies of 8 billion yuan (about 5% of total state revenues).[2]

The new prices were calculated so that the average price of grain remained roughly constant. However, some farmers, who had rapidly expanded their above-quota marketings in recent years, did suffer a reduction in income, while other farmers must have benefited. But the more important impact of the price changes was that the marginal price of grain was lowered for everyone. For the farmer making a decision about the allocation of his land, fertilizer, and effort between grain and some competing crop or activity, it is only the marginal price that matters, and the lowering of the marginal price of grain inevitably led to a relative decrease in the emphasis farmers put on grain growing. This was all the more true in that the shift to a contract system was accompanied by a decrease in the amount of extra-economic compulsion to grow grain. Peasants had somewhat more freedom to base their decisions on purely economic considerations; since every indication is that grain growing remains far less lucrative than most economic crops, peasants naturally put less stress on grain. The pull away from grain production was intensified by the proliferation of income earning opportunities in the countryside. Policy continued to encourage peasants to engage in lucrative sideline activities—transport, construction, and petty trade—as an alternative to crop raising. Moreover, the decontrol of nonstaple food (discussed below) increased the attractiveness of alternatives to grain production, such as growing vegetables or raising pigs or poultry.

The consequences of these policy changes became manifest during 1985. After three straight years of good weather, agricultural production in 1985 once again suffered from adverse weather. The most striking losses were those caused by a series of storms and floods in East China, and particularly in the three northeastern provinces. In the northeast, it was estimated that adverse weather led to a reduction in grain output of about 10 million metric tons. Nationally, in marked contrast to the situation in the previous year, per acre grain yields declined, and this combined with a continuing decline in the acreage sown to grain (over 3% in 1985) to result in a decline in grain output of 28 million tons. In absolute terms, this was the largest year to year decline in PRC history, and the percentage decline (7%) was surpassed only in the crisis years 1959 and 1960. Output of other crops (such as oilseeds, sugar cane, and tobacco) continued to expand, however, and the total value of agricultural output increased by 3%.

Industry and Finance

The economic reforms enacted during the last quarter of 1984 primarily affected the operations of the industrial and financial system. A full accounting of these reforms is beyond the scope of the present paper,[3] but the common feature of all the reform measures was that they gave industrial and commercial enterprises substantially more freedom of operation than in the past. Correspondingly, the banking system was given greater freedom to respond to the demands of the industrial system. The result was a tremendous increase in economic activity, fueled by an even greater increase in the effective demand for goods and services.

On the consumption side, expansion of enterprise autonomy during 1984 gave factories and other units substantially more control over their wage payments than previously. Ceilings on bonus payments were eliminated in most areas, and factories were encouraged to experiment with a variety of schemes linking wage payments and—for the first time since the 1950s—promotions to increases in profitability. Not surprisingly, factories responded to these newfound freedoms by passing out healthy wage and bonus increases to their employees. In the final quarter of 1984, total bonus outlays were 117% higher than in the final quarter of 1983, and in the first quarter of 1985, bonuses were 99% higher than in the equivalent period a year earlier.[4]

On the investment side, factories responded to their newfound freedoms with a tremendous burst of new construction. Overall in 1984, state fixed investment had increased by 24%, and the pace of increase accelerated into the first part of 1985. Preliminary figures (which generally do not count all investment) indicated that fixed investment was up 43.5% in the first six months of 1985, compared to the same period in 1984. A new "leap forward," stimulated by the surge of economic reform, was clearly in the making.

In order to understand this enormous expansion in investment, it is necessary to look at some of the changes in the banking system. China's economic reforms clearly envision a greater role for the banking system, as it is expected that bank loans will gradually replace budgetary grants as the main form of investment throughout the economy. In 1984, steps were taken to give the various constituent parts of the banking system more independence, in order to give local banks more of a voice in determining loan decisions. The various functional bank systems—the Agricultural Bank, the Industrial-Commercial Bank, and the Bank of China (primarily a foreign exchange bank)—were authorized to compete with each other in making loans. Moreover, a new system was devised in which local banks that successfully attracted more deposits would be able to make more loans of all kinds. In order to put this system on an "automatic" basis, it was decreed that the basis from which increased loans would be allowed would be the volume of outstanding loans at year-end 1984. It was thought that these changes would give local banks a much greater interest in finding good "customers" for their loans.

In fact, these measures gave banks an enormous incentive to expand lending to the maximum possible extent. The greater the volume of loans outstanding at year-end 1984, the greater authority a local bank would have to make loans in future years. Moreover, these incentives were combined with a general slackening of the degree of central government supervision of bank lending. The government gives local banks an annual quota for maximum lending in a given year, but in most years this quota is not particularly strict. Banks that make loans above their quota are rarely reprimanded, as long as they can argue that their additional loans were required for legitimate purposes. In 1984 and early 1985, banks had especially strong incentives to exceed their quotas, and worry later about justifying their actions to higher authorities. Moreover, in this activity, local banks had strong support from local government leaders. A whole group of new provincial leaders had come to power in 1983 and 1984, and these leaders clearly understood that the way to make their mark in the new China was to accelerate the pace of economic development in their own provinces. This leadership actively urged their local banks to expand lending for new construction projects, and as the banks were only too ready to succumb to this pressure, lending activity accelerated rapidly.[5] By year-end 1984, loans to state industry for both current operations and fixed investment were up 48%; loans to urban collective and individual businesses 85%; and loans to rural enterprises from the banks increased 96%, while loans from the rural credit cooperatives increased 125%.

The banking system was creating new monetary assets at a remarkable pace, and the liberalization of the economic system gave factories unprecedented freedom to sped the monetary assets they received from the banks. It was this surge of purchasing power that fueled the spectacular industrial growth of early 1985. Enterprises, awash with liquidity, aggressively purchased materials needed for production and new construction; and in the face of vigorous demand for nearly all products, factories rapidly stepped up their own production. A surge of purchasing power was thus occurring simultaneously in every sphere of the economy. Just as factories were expanding investment, the combination of a rich harvest and healthy wage increases in the urban sector was rapidly increasing household purchasing power. By the end of 1984, currency in circulation had increased by a whopping 48%.

Markets and Prices

After four years of moderate economic policies, China at the beginning of 1985 thus moved suddenly into a situation in which powerful inflationary pressures had been created in the economy. The increased demand created rapid increases in real output, but also created serious strains on the economic structure. The gains to this high-pressure, high-growth strategy, in terms of expanded output, are fairly obvious. However, the losses, though less apparent, are no less real, and deserve further discussion.

Although the supply of output was expanding rapidly, it could not possibly increase as rapidly as the demand for these goods. As a result, a "seller's market" was created for a wide range of goods, in which producers could sell nearly any output, regardless of the quality or price. An immediate result was a substantial decline in the quality of output across the board. A chorus of complaints from both consumers and producing enterprises arose about the deterioration of quality.[6] Moreover, output of different commodities did not expand at an equal pace. In particular, bottlenecks like those in energy supply (particularly electricity and petroleum) were intensified, and transportation services could not keep up with rapidly expanding demand. With so many customers competing for these bottleneck commodities, each individual customer found it increasingly difficult to arrange an uninterrupted supply of basic materials. Most handicapped were the large, priority state projects. These projects, concentrated in just those sectors (energy and transport) where long-run development is most needed, make up the core of the shrunken, but still important, state-planned economy. These projects are still built into the network of state planning, but increasingly supplies have been diverted to those willing to pay higher market prices. As a result, the rate of fulfillment of delivery contracts within the state plan for crucial materials like steel and cement declined to 88% and 93% respectively in the first quarter of 1985, from around 97% in 1984. While electricity blackouts became increasingly common, the share of completed capital construction investment devoted to energy projects declined by three percentage points. (However, an increased share of investment went for transportation projects.)[7]

Finally, given the liberalized economic environment, inflationary pressures increasingly erupted into open inflation. Inflation is an important social issue in contemporary China: it is also a problem that cannot be addressed in isolation from the larger questions of economic reform. For many years in China prices have been controlled by the state, and effectively frozen. While some adjustments have taken place in recent years, the pace of change—particularly for consumer goods—had been slow until 1985. An effective economic reform program requires that prices play a much more active role: that prices, in short, fluctuate to equate supply and demand, and allow producers to make rational decisions independently of the state planning apparatus. Relaxing state control over prices is made more difficult by the fact that certain consumer prices—above all, food prices—have been set for years at a price substantially below the actual cost of supplying urban dwellers. If prices are to be freed, the cost of food to urbanites will inevitably increase. In order to manage this politically sensitive issue, the Chinese government decided to go ahead in 1985 with a simultaneous program of increasing workers' wages and decontrolling the price of foods other than grain. Such a move was designed to transfer subsidies given to the commercial system into overt wage increases, and allow the market to play a role in determining production and sales. Each wage earner was given a monthly wage increase (7 *yuan* in Beijing) as compensation for the expected increase in prices. Thus, it was the intention of China's leadership to carry out a "managed" inflation, taking place in a single step without reducing the real income of urbanites.

This reform was carried out in most of China during the second quarter of 1985, and could hardly have come at a worse time. Precisely at this time, the flood of increased income that had been building since late 1984 was at its peak: Excess demand for a range of commodities meant that as soon as price controls were relaxed, upward pressure on prices was converted into real price increases. Open inflation set off a chorus of protest, as workers saw their recent wage gains eroded, and planners were forced to scale back projected price liberalization in the face of this political pressure. It is difficult to determine just how much inflation reduced the real income gains of Chinese urbanites in 1985. Official Chinese figures show a rise in the urban cost of living for all of 1985 of 11.9%, but this probably understates the full magnitude of the inflation. Inflation in Beijing is generally conceded to have run around 20%, and although food price increases have been more severe in the largest cities, the national figure may not be much below this. The average urban wage—including all subsidies provided for price increases—increased by 17.2%, while *per capita* urban incomes recorded in household budget surveys (which reflect changes in labor force participation and income from individual businesses, as well as sampling error) increased 23.8%. Thus, accepting official figures on the rate of inflation would yield increases in real wages and real urban incomes of 5.3% and 11.9% respectively. The most that can be said with assurance is that inflation ate up the majority of workers' wage gains, but probably not the totality.

Whatever the precise figures on inflation, the fear of further fueling inflation led the Chinese leadership to scale back the program of price liberalization originally intended. Thus, textile prices were briefly decontrolled during the first part of the year, but controls were reimposed when the magnitude of inflationary pressures became evident. In Beijing, the original plan had been to raise fares on the heavily subsidized bus network, but this touchy issue was shelved in the course of the year. The most sensitive measure had been the decontrol of pork prices, but in order to prevent the price of pork from skyrocketing, planners felt compelled to reinstitute subsidies for pork retailers, in exchange for price restraint (at least in Beijing). Thus the plan to put pork on a purely market basis failed, while consumer complaints about deteriorating quality multiplied.[8]

An analogous situation prevailed in the market for producers' goods. A unique feature of China's economic reform strategy has been the decision to allow a series of "secondary markets" for goods that do not go directly into consumption. Independent purchase and sale of producers' goods, which would be illegal in most planned economies, have been permitted and even encouraged in China. In these secondary markets, goods are sold at prices that approximate the free market prices. Thus, there exist two prices for every good: A state-set price, typically low and fixed, is used for in-plan transactions, and a free market price, typically much higher and fluctuating according to supply and demand, is used in other transactions. One of the most important components in the expansion of enterprise autonomy during late 1984 was the across-the-board freedom given to enterprises to market outside-of-plan output on the market. This led to a rapid expansion in the proportion of output sold independently by enterprises. During the first half of 1985, one-third of state industrial output in the largest cities was sold independently by enterprises.[9]

This decision was part of a larger strategy of reform. Rather than readjusting prices administratively through the planned economy, Chinese planners were hoping to simply let the market play a more and more important role in production decisions, until it gradually usurped many of the functions of the planners. Planners would gradually gain experience in operating in the marketplace, while protecting their priority projections from disruption; in time, planned prices would be adjusted with reference to market prices, and the economy would be guided towards a socialist market economy, as planned and market prices came together. Instead, given the inflationary environment in 1985, the reverse happened: Demand pressures pushed market prices further and further from plan prices. A standardized steel product, 6.5 mm. rebar, can serve as an example: At the beginning of the year the market price was 1,375 yuan per ton, nearly twice the state-set price of 700 yuan. However, the market price climbed steadily through the year, finally settling at a range between 1,700 and 2,000 yuan by September.[10] Thus, instead of being gradually unified, the planned and market sectors gradually grew further apart.

Economic Controls

In this situation, it was inevitable that planners would take steps to re-establish macroeconomic balance. Voices were raised criticizing overly rapid growth in February, but the first remedial measures were not taken until March. Action was precipitated by a drastic depletion of China's foreign exchange reserves. The same set of reform measures that permitted expanded wage payments and investment had also liberalized access to foreign currency. Local governments and enterprises responded with an orgy of foreign buying to equip their new investment projects; morever, the general laxity extended to purchases of imported consumption goods as well. Imports to China surged, while China's reserve stocks of foreign exchange plummeted. From a high of 16 billion U.S. dollars in September 1984, reserves declined to 11 billion in March 1985, with every indication of continuing drawdowns in the future. Just at this point, a major scandal broke in Hainan Island, when it was revealed that local authorities had been importing massive quantities of Japanese automobiles and reselling them, at a healthy profit, throughout China. This situation finally precipitated drastic measures. The head of the central bank was removed, and replaced by the political stalwart Chen Muhua. Chen's first move was to drastically recentralize control over foreign exchange. Local governments were forced to cut back imports, reneging on some agreements, and disrupting foreign trade relations. Even so, China ran a trade deficit for all of 1985 of U.S. $15 billion: besides drawing down reserves, the deficit was financed by a $3.5 billion surplus in invisibles, and the absorption of $4.3 billion in foreign investment.

Chen's initiative signalled the beginning of a series of steps taken through the banking system, aiming to reestablish contol over domestic finances, and thereby over the whole economy. Quotas on bank lending were lowered and—more significantly—it became a key tenet of government policy that these quotas were to be respected under all circumstances. Regulation of wage payments was stepped up, and bank supervision of enterprise bonuses was greatly intensified. The growth rate of bonuses began to decline: measured in relation to the same period a year previously, bonuses grew by 45.2% in the second quarter; 13.6% in the third quarter; and actually declined by 34.7% in September.[11] Needless to say, bonus reductions in the face of open inflation did not prove popular.

Initially, these moves through the banking system had little impact on industrial investment or production. Enterprises had accumulated such enormous financial resources that a reduction in new lending made little difference: For the first half of the year, enterprises simply drew down abundant bank balances to continue their investment projects, and overall investment continued to grow. Moreover, the new bank stringency ran into immediate opposition from the local political leaders who had been enthusiastic proponents of the initial overexpansion of bank credit. As local leaders maneuvered to protect their favorite local projects, they found it relatively easy to put pressure on the local banks. For instance, in the city of Xian, the vice-mayor called a meeting of local bank heads, and explained to them that he needed an additional 9 million yuan in order to complete the city's investment programs: Until the bankers agreed to provide it, he indicated, the meeting would not be adjourned. It is not recorded how long the meeting continued, but in the end the vice-mayor got his money.[12]

This situation was not overcome until, at the beginning of July, Deng Xiaoping acknowledged that the torrid pace of growth in the first half of the year contained "unhealthy elements." From this point, the attitude of the party apparatus began to change: It became a matter of both party and governmental policy to reduce the scale of investment and slow the rate of output growth. From July, the pace of both began to slacken: A familiar stress on party discipline and administrative controls gradually brought investment back under control. During the third quarter, localities were instructed to halt investment growth, and eliminate all new out-of-budget investment projects.[13] By September, the annual rate of industrial growth was brought down to 15%, and fourth quarter growth was around 10%. Thus, every indication is that the government, relying primarily on administrative controls, was able to bring the economy back to a reasonable growth rate relatively rapidly.

Conclusions

It is not easy to make an overall assessment of economic performance when such drastic changes in economic policy follow one another so closely. However, a few outstanding features deserve comment. First, Chinese policymakers made several important mistakes in late 1984 and 1985. These mistakes include the reduction of grain purchasing prices; inappropriate reforms in the banking system, especially at the end of 1984; and poor timing of price reform measures. The most fundamental error, however, was failing to recognize at the beginning of 1985 that the economy was already overheated and required remedial measures. Instead, through most of the first half of 1985, party leaders were stressing the overall favorable situation, and emphasizing the importance of the strategic goal of quadrupling output by the year 2000. This created an atmosphere of "leaping forward" that was disturbingly similar to periods in China's past when rapid growth was stressed above all else.

Obviously, the mentality created and reinforced through the party apparatus made it nearly impossible to rectify the real problems that were emerging.

As a result, China's ongoing reform process suffered some real setbacks during 1985. The failure of the banking system effectively to regulate the economy struck an ominous note, since it indicated the immaturity of the economic mechanisms that will be relied on to guide the economy in the future. The partial failure of price reform was also disappointing. Not only was public support for further price reforms undermined by the magnitude of inflationary pressures, but the reimposition of administrative controls on prices in some areas meant that the intended benefits were not fully realized. In the immediate future, the necessity of using administrative controls to limit the scope of investment inevitably means that further reform in that area will be delayed. Furthermore, continuing inflationary pressures have caused the leadership to declare that there will be no more major price reforms in the coming year. On another level, the reform-oriented leadership suffered a major blow to its prestige due to the accumulation of errors in economic policymaking, and this will inevitably slow the progress of reform in the immediate future.

The events of 1985 provide evidence of the continuing difficulties China's planners have in controlling the economy. Nearly every key economic magnitude was out of control in the early part of 1985—investment, household income, imports, and money supply all grew at a rate far beyond that which planners had intended. Yet while overall investment was far greater than planners desired, priority state projects suffered from shortages and delays. One statistic can illustrate the magnitude of the difficulties planners are having. The Sixth Five Year Plan, promulgated only in September 1982, called for the completion of 400 large and medium-sized construction projects by the end of 1985. Through the end of 1984, 399 such projects had in fact been completed—but of these, only 197 had been included in the plan: More than half the completed projects were outside the plan.[14] An additional 97 large and medium-sized projects were completed during 1985, but of course not all these will have been included in the five-year plan either. This pattern—overall growth well above the plan, combined with failure to complete specific planned objectives—has come to characterize the Chinese economy.

In large part, this pattern is caused by the partially reformed character of the Chinese economy. Financial and material resources for investment have been widely decentralized, but because planners have been unable to regulate these resources effectively through economic means (such as interest rates or taxation), recurrent episodes of excess investment require planners to reimpose administrative controls on investment. This imposes a "stop and go" character on the investment process which must have a harmful effect on efficiency. Moreover, it is always easier for smaller investment projects to evade administrative controls; as a result, the average size of Chinese investments has been shrinking steadily in recent years. In some cases, it may be efficient to forego large, expensive projects in favor of smaller, incremental investments; but in other cases, adoption of advanced technology dictates a minimum scale which is rarely attained in Chinese construction projects. Given the weak control of central planners and the still inadequate role for well functioning markets, there is no clear way to determine the appropriate scale of investment projects.

The picture emerging from 1985 is not all negative. The industrial output gains registered were not illusory, even if the pace of growth will be difficult to sustain in the future. Real growth was sufficiently rapid to create a substantial increase in budgetary revenues, allowing the government to balance its budget for the first time since 1979. Moreover, even with the failure of some aspects of price reform, a measure of price flexibility has been introduced into the economy that is generally healthy, and flourishing markets for farm produce attest to the successes that have been achieved in that area. By the end of the year, there were even a few indications that the administrative regulation of the economy had achieved success more rapidly than anticipated, and that further modest price reforms might after all be considered in 1986.

The counterpart to the failure to complete large-scale planned construction has been the strong growth of small-scale production. This is most apparent in the extraordinarily rapid expansion of the rural industrial sector. Pulled forward by vigorous demand and easy access to bank credit in the early part of the year, rural industries responded with spectacular increases in output. Some of this expanded output came precisely in those areas—such as coal and building materials—which are critically needed in China's economy. Moreover, this sector seems to have enough vitality that the sudden clampdown on bank credit by midyear has not done more than moderate a growth rate that remains extremely high. Protected by wage rates that remain substantially below those in state-run industry, this sector has been vigorously growing in an economic environment that is primarily dominated by market considerations. Moreover, state-run factories, especially the smaller ones, are also beginning to orient their activities much more toward market conditions. Further economic success depends on whether this vitality can be extended to China's larger enterprises, either through an improved planning system or through further extension of market relationships—

or through some combination of both. China's industrial development depends on the future evolution of this extraordinary and precarious situation.

Notes

1. Unless otherwise noted, statistics on economic performance are derived from the following sources: For 1984 year-end data, *1985 Zhongguo Tongji Nianjian;* for 1985 monthly and quarterly data, *Zhongguo Tongji Yuebao* 1985:11; and for 1985 full-year figures, State Statistical Bureau, "Statistical Report on the National Economy and Social Development in 1985," *Renmin Ribao,* March 1, 1986, p. 2.

2. *Jingjixue Zhoubao,* November 24, 1985, p. 1.

3. For a fuller account, see B. Naughton, "Finance and Planning Reforms in Industry," in U.S. Congress Joint Economic Committee, ed., *China's Economy in the 1980s* (Washington, D.C.: Government Printing Office, 1986).

4. Yu Naidong and Teng Juixiong, "Strive to consolidate achievements," *Zhongguo Jinrong* 1985:12, p. 35.

5. "Third Session of China Capital Construction Economics Research Society," *Jingjixue Dongtai* 1985:11, pp. 16–18.

6. See "The trend towards declining quality in our city is being controlled," *Beijing Ribao,* October 12, 1985, p. 1.

7. Dai Guanlai, "A few problems of the extra-plan prices of means of production," *Jingjixue Dongtai* 1985:9, p. 25; see also "Third Session . . ."

8. Zhou Pengnian, "Reform must raise the ability to respond to changing circumstances," *Jingji Cankao,* October 16, 1985, p. 6; Interview with Zhang Zhuoyuan, head of the Finance and Trade Economic Research Institute, Beijing, November 30, 1985.

9. "Industrial enterprises in 48 cities: Accelerated turnover and higher profits," *Jingji Ribao,* September 11, 1985, p. 2. The national proportion would be higher, since rural enterprises and those in smaller cities tend to be less tightly integrated into the planning system.

10. Prices are given by Dai Guanlai; and in various issues of *Wuzi Guanli* and *Wuhan Shichang Wujia Xinxi.*

11. Yu Naidong and Teng Huixiong.

12. "Party and government leaders in some regions compel banks to make loans," *Zhongguo Jinrong* 1985:9, p. 7.

13. "Construction Expenditures Under Fire," *China Daily,* October 3, 1985, p. 3.

14. "Implementation conditions for our sixth Five Year Plan are excellent," *Jingji Ribao,* September 9, 1985, p.1.

5
Education

Peter J. Seybolt

1985 was the most important year for education in China in nearly two decades. The "Guiding Principles" for the Seventh Five Year Plan, 1986–1990, passed by the National Representative Congress of the Communist Party of China (September 23, 1985), stipulated unequivocally that in the future education must be considered as serious a concern as economic construction, and that indeed success in one was contingent on success in the other.[1] The ambitious economic goals announced by Party Secretary Hu Yaobang are to quadruple total industrial and agricultural output value by the end of the 20th Century; to make China a relatively developed country by the year 2021, when the Communist Party celebrates its centenary; and to create a "first-class prosperous and powerful nation by 2049," the centenary of the founding of the People's Republic of China.[2] These goals are considered impossible to attain unless the educational level of the nation is raised substantially.

Almost all discussion of education reform in China in 1985 refers primarily to the economic benefits of better schooling. There is, to be sure, considerable discussion of socialist morality, warning youth to beware of the corrupting influence of certain bourgeois values and practices but the former Maoist insistence on the social transformation role of education is as absent as the Western liberal bias toward self-fulfillment. Economic development may not be an end in itself for China's current leaders, but it is the major concern of current education reform.

That being the case, recently compiled statistics give rise to a sense of urgency. According to a 10% sample survey of the 1982 official census in China, 78% of the industrial labor force had a ninth grade education or less; 7.9% had little or no education; 20.4% had a secondary education; and only 1.6% had graduated from universities and colleges. In the eight grade technical scale applied to Chinese industries, the census indicated that 71% of the workers were in the lowest three grades and only 2% were in the top two grades.[3]

In the agrarian sector of the economy, the educational level is much lower. The overwhelming majority of the rural populace have less than a full elementary school education, and at least 80 million young and middle aged farmers have little or no education. Among older farmers the situation is worse. China's current attempt to modernize agriculture in order to get the most from its meager endowment of arable land (.11 hectare per capita, only 40% of the world's average) is thwarted by the fact that there are only four agro-technicians per 10,000 rural populace.[4]

The greatest loss of productive potential due to inadequate education reflects the persistence of traditional Chinese attitudes toward females. The 1982 census sample indicates that only 51.1% of females fifteen years of age and older have attended primary school compared to 79.1% of males. And only 8.3% of females, compared to 13.3% of males, have finished secondary school. Changing attitudes and greater attention to education of both sexes is apparent when the age group is broken down by decades. Of the youth from 15 to 24 years old, 82.2% of the females and 95.1% of the males are reported by the census sample to have attended primary school, but discrimination is still apparent.[5]

Overall, Chinese and World Bank statistics indicate that in the early 1980s about 90% of school age children entered primary school, 60% completed it, but only 30% graduated with a performance that was up to standard.[6] That is cause for considerable concern to a nation that aspires to the goals articulated by Party General Secretary Hu Yaobang.

The disparity between goals and aspirations in China should not be allowed to obscure the remarkable accomplishments in education there since the establishment of the People's Republic in 1949. Primary school enrollment has increased five and a half times from 24.39 million in 1949 to 135.78 million in 1983. For secondary schools the increase is from 1.27 to 46.28 million and in tertiary schools from 117,000 to 1,756,000.[7] Between 1949 and 1985, 400 million students have graduated from elementary schools and over 250 million from junior secondary schools. The literacy rate has increased from about 20% in 1949 to about 80% in 1985 according to Chinese official estimates.[8]

Compared to other less developed countries, these achievements have been noteworthy, particularly at the primary and secondary levels. The World Bank 1985 special report on education in China (based on weeks of on-site investigation) begins with the statement: "China's achievements in education since 1949 have been unmatched among developing countries of the same income level. Enrollments in formal and nonformal primary and secondary education have been high by any standards." It goes on to mention, however, that "Manpower shortages, affecting industry, agriculture, transportation, and other economic sectors, have hampered the achievement of the four modernizations. Accompanying shortages of qualified manpower has been an abundance of unqualified workers and staff at several levels, leading to low efficiency in enterprises, and also in education."[9]

The National Education Conference, the New Education Commission, and the Decision on Education Reform

Recognition of these problems provided impetus in China for a major study of education from October 1984 to May 1985, involving over 10,000 specialists from various disciplines. It culminated in a report intended to provide guidelines for education for many years. That report, "The Decision of the Chinese Communist Party Central Committee on Reform of the Education System" was drafted and revised eleven times before presentation at a National Education Conference on May 19, 1985.[10]

The National Education Conference is now regarded as a major turning point for education in China. It was attended by the leading Party and government officials whose presence, and whose remarks, confirmed the essential message that education is too important to be left solely to educators. Deng Xiaoping, addressing the delegates criticized officials at all levels who "lack a sense of urgency" about education. "Leaders who neglect education are immature leaders" he said. "They lack a long view and are therefore incapable of leading the modernization program."[11]

The comprehensive importance of education for all endeavors was recognized institutionally shortly after the close of the National Education Conference. In June 1985 the Ministry of Education was abolished and replaced by a National Education Commission having considerably broader powers. The old Ministry of Education had restricted jurisdiction. It was one of numerous ministries and agencies of equal rank, many of which had their own education programs and institutions. There were no unified guidelines and little coordination of effort except in a loose and ineffectual way through the State Council. The new National Education Commission is superior to the ministries and has jurisdiction over them. It is one of only six Commissions directly under the State Council. It is headed by Vice Premier Li Peng, a key member of the State Council and generally considered to be a leading candidate to succeed Zhao Ziyang as Premier. Its main charge is not only to centralize and coordinate policy formation and implementation at the top, but also to oversee decentralization of direct administration at lower levels. The Commission will issue general guidelines. Officials at lower levels, and even in individual institutions, will have unprecedented authority to decide how to manage their particular affairs. The emphasis on managerial decentralization is explicit in the principal product of the National Education Conference: The "Decision on Education Reform."

The "Decision" builds on the many education reforms since 1979 that have negated or reversed the values and practices of the Cultural Revolution period. It stipulates three major areas for special attention:

1. Transference of responsibility for developing basic education to local areas, and implementation, step-by-step, of a nine year compulsory education system.
2. Reorganization of the structure of secondary education, with particular attention to the development of vocational and technical education.
3. Reformation, in institutions of higher education, of procedure for admission and for post-graduation job allocation, and expansion of management authority in the individual schools.[12]

Local Government Responsibility and the Plan for Nine Years of Compulsory Education

The plan for nine years of compulsory education breaks the population into three major categories, and implementation into three stages. The first category includes roughly 25% of the population who live in cities, coastal provinces and a few inland areas where population is most concentrated and the economy is relatively developed. Many of these areas already have compulsory education through the ninth grade. The others are expected to achieve it by 1990.

The second category encompasses the 50% of the population who live in towns and rural areas where economic development is moderate. By 1995, those areas are expected to universalize elementary and junior secondary schooling.

The third category includes the remaining 25% of the population who live in economically backward areas, many of which are sparsely populated, and geographically remote. In those areas, progress will be uneven depending on local circumstances. No completion date has been set.

The "Decision" also gives unprecedented (in China) attention to a much smaller, fourth category of the population—the blind, deaf-mutes, disabled, and mentally handicapped, and admonishes local areas to make greater efforts on their behalf.[13] There has been very little attention given this category in the past, with some notable exceptions.[14]

Management

Responsibility for implementing the nine year compulsory education policy rests largely with the administrative units subordinate to the central government (provinces, municipalities, autonomous areas) and their sub-units (counties, townships, villages, etc.). The only change from the past in this regard is that directives from the central government will be less detailed and explicit, and the division of labor and responsibility between the various levels of government will be left to each area (province, etc.) to decide. The emphasis is on increased devolution of decision-making and financing to lower levels accompanied by a strong admonition to innovate. In other words, the trend is toward increasingly locally run schools.

The typical pattern that is emerging, according to a recent article,[15] is as follows: Provinces are responsible for general implementation policies and for distributing funds from the central government to the counties. In addition they directly administer a few key secondary schools and experimental schools. Counties adapt provincial guidelines to local conditions, distribute funds to townships, and directly manage senior secondary schools, teacher training schools and in-service teacher training, agricultural vocational schools, key primary and junior secondary schools, and some of the regular primary and secondary schools. The rest are managed by the township governments (comparable to the former communes). Many schools under township supervision are popular-management (*minban*) schools. Cooperatively owned at the local level (i.e., not by the state government), they receive very little funding from the county and are responsible for providing their own teachers, facilities and so on. The *minban* schools tend to have the worst facilities, the poorest teachers and the highest drop-out rate. Schools that are not *minban*, that is, those owned by the state are classified in two categories, "regular" and "key."

Key Schools

The so-called key schools (literally "concentration point schools") are a relatively few, select institutions that receive superior funding, equipment, teaching staff and students. The obvious problems of inequity and inequality that such schools pose for a government committed to socialism made them anathema during the Cultural Revolution, and they continue to be controversial today. The current justification for affirming their existence is that it is necessary to concentrate scarce resources to produce the expertise required for effective pursuit of the "four modernizations"; and furthermore that they set the standard and provide a model for other schools. Critics dismiss those contentions, arguing that the economic base will be weakened eventually if majority interests are sacrificed for those of the minority; and furthermore that the emulation model justification is specious, given the meager resources of regular schools.

Criticism of the key school concept in the past few years has altered some of its more extreme manifestations at the lower education levels. Key elementary schools, especially in urban areas where they are most prevalent, now draw mainly from their local area, rather than from the whole city, and have thus become less elite. Key classes in regular elementary schools, which were initiated a few years ago, have now been eliminated due to the perception that they unduly discriminate against regular students, making them lose interest in schooling, and increasing their drop-out rate. The total number of key schools has also been reduced so that now only about 1% of elementary and 4% of secondary schools throughout the country are designated key. Students attending them (and key classes on the secondary level) comprise perhaps 5% of the total student body.[16] The percentages in urban areas are much higher than in rural areas.

Funding

From the beginning, one of the main reasons for key schools has been a concern with financing education. Proponents of key schools argue that it is necessary to concentrate scarce resources, material and human, where they will most immediately contribute to the goal of rapid modernization. The Cultural Revolution concern with equality is to be deferred until material conditions provide the possibility for something more than an equality of poverty. Inequity will have to increase before it can be reduced according to current thinking. The validity of that proposition can be debated, especially in light of information on current funding practices.

China spends less on education, as a percentage of GNP, than almost any country in the world. In the early 1980s, it allocated only about 3% of public and private funds to education, compared with a median of 4–5% in other developing countries, and 6% or much higher in economically advanced countries. As a percentage of total government allocation, China spent 7.1% on education in 1982 and has increased the percentage since, but still has not reached the median of 15.5% in other developing countries and 15% in advanced countries. Expenditure per student is also lower in China than elsewhere. It has greatly increased in the past several years to the equivalent of about U.S. $50–$52, but that does not approach the approximately U.S. $80 spent on average in the 65 other low-income countries with which China is most suitably compared.[17]

The government of China does take more responsibility for economic, social and cultural concerns of the populace than most countries, which must be taken into consideration, but that does not entirely account for the disparity. Nor does it explain why China has done so much better than other developing countries in providing education for its citizens. The answer lies principally in the fact that, on the one hand, there has been greater political commitment and control than elsewhere, and on the other, very little has been spent on teacher's salaries and on facilities, especially in rural areas. Given the current emphasis on education, both political commitment and funding for the personnel and facilities will increase in the future. The two are closely related, indeed contingent. Funding, as before, will come principally from the local areas and will depend on the degree of political commitment emanating from the top. The "Decision on Education Reform" calls for transference to positions of greater authority those who demonstrate enthusiasm for the new policies. Deng Xiaoping has admonished officials at all levels to visit schools, note their needs, and help them solve problems. Since publication of the "Decision," most provinces and municipalities have held special education meetings in which they pledged greater support for education.[18] Among the first funding priorities is to raise teacher salaries.

Teachers and Other Resources

Teaching is the lowest paid profession in China. Elementary and secondary school teachers are among the lowest paid of any employed group, especially teachers working in the popular-management (*minban*) schools in the countryside. An investigation in May 1985 in a county in Hebei Province revealed that only 5 of 44 teachers in local village schools in one township had been paid on time. Most had not been paid at all so far that year, and two had not been paid in 1984. Two others were owed salaries from late 1982 and one from the end of 1981. Adding to their economic woes the *minban* teachers are denied the economic benefits, such as free medical care, granted to teachers and other personnel hired by the state.[19]

It follows that the social status and the morale of teachers in general, and of rural teachers especially, is very low. A recent article comments that "they are often insulted, and in extreme cases suffer beatings at the hands of their tormentors." The article also notes, without explanation, that children of teachers often find it difficult to get good jobs.[20]

It is not surprising that many of the most able teachers leave the classroom for other jobs, and that many graduates of teacher training institutions, both secondary and tertiary levels, never go into teaching. A recent graduate of the prestigious, key, East China Teacher's University was quoted as saying, "80% of us don't want to be teachers. Teachers are still looked down on. . . . Most of us tried our best to find other jobs."[21] Such desires for alternative occupation are often obliged by government authorities. In Hubei Province, for example, half of the 2,000–3,000 yearly graduates of the province's eleven teacher training institutes, and half of the teachers assigned to the province by the state, are reassigned to other work by provincial and city authorities. An article in the *People's Daily* commented, "They keep the better graduates for themselves. As a result the county schools are given two or three new teachers each, despite thousands of new pupil-enrollments annually. Many of the new staff have poor health or low qualifications. . . ."[22]

These problems have been addressed by a series of measures since the issuance of the "Decision on Education Reform." September 10 was declared "Teacher's Day," to be recognized annually by a public celebration, forums and symposia, and awards to outstanding teachers. It is the first such day since the establishment of the People's Republic. The declared purpose is to focus the nation's attention on education. More substantially, the government has declared a continuing salary adjustment that will raise teachers' salaries 5 yuan per month above raises in other professions. The process is to begin by granting salary raises six months earlier for teachers than for clerks or cadres.[23] Presumably this does not directly affect the *minban* teachers, who are not on the government payroll, but they will be helped in other ways. Township governments have been told to use a majority of their revenue for education[24] and all levels of government have been strongly urged to increase funding for education and allocate special funds to repair and improve teachers' housing, provide medical services, honor back-pay obligations, and raise salaries. According to one report, huge sums have already been pledged for this purpose. Factories and other economic units have been encouraged to run schools for children of their employees and others in the local area. Collectives and self-employed individuals are urged to donate money to local schools.[25]

Another effort to give special aid to remote and impoverished areas was dramatized recently when Party General Secretary Hu Yaobang, with great publicity, gave a send-off speech to 3250 young people chosen from central Party and government departments to go to backward areas in 22 provinces and autonomous regions to help train teachers. Hu invoked the idealism of other youth to follow their example.[26] Those who do, especially graduates of teacher training institutes, are given special pay and the promise of good jobs when they return to the cities several years later. A long term provision is the increasing tendency to recruit people from rural areas for teacher training institutions with the understanding that they will serve in the countryside upon graduation.

Special admissions allotments for such students gives them advantages such as lower admissions standards.

The problem of inadequate facilities is also receiving a lot of attention. It is a separate issue, but not unrelated to that of teacher welfare if a report in the *China Daily* is representative. The report states that 28% of all the elementary and secondary schools in the nation's capital rent space to other units for non-educational use. Three hundred forty-nine schools have rented 92,000 square meters of space, sometimes for ten year leases, in order to provide welfare funds for teachers and staff.[27] The problem is even greater in the countryside where often education facilities are requisitioned for other uses. That practice is now supposed to stop.

The other major measure being taken to improve education in both urban and rural areas is in-service teacher-training through short-term courses at universities, colleges and secondary schools, night schools, correspondence and television courses and so on. The need is apparent in a 1983 government estimate that 48% of the 5.4 million elementary school teachers were unqualified. Other reports put the proportion as high as two-thirds.[28]

Student Enrollment

A considerable amount of the recent literature on education reform calls for increasing the enrollment in teacher training institutions to meet current needs. For instance, He Dongchang, Vice Director of the new Education Commission, and former director of the Ministry of Education, cites a need to train two million teachers, in addition to the eight million now teaching at the primary and secondary levels, in the next five years. In addition, he said that 500,000 teachers currently in service must be trained each year to bring them up to standard.[29] World Bank analysts argue, on the other hand, that the issue is one of quality and efficient use rather than numbers. Student enrollment has actually decreased substantially in the past several years due to the nation's new economic policies, and will continue to decrease for many years as the effects of China's stringent birth control policy are felt.[30]

Elementary school enrollment reached a peak of 150,940,000 in 1975 according to recent Ministry of Education figures. It declined to 135,780,000 in 1983 and probably to around 124,000,000 in 1985. A World Bank study projects a continuing decline until 1995 when the elementary school student population will be approximately 88 million and then will climb to 95 million and level off by the end of the century as efforts to universalize education take effect.[31]

Secondary school enrollment continued to climb after the disruptions in the early years of the Cultural Revolution, growing from 20,250,000 in 1969 to a peak of 68,490,000 in 1977, and then declining to 46,280,000 in 1983 as many of the secondary schools established during the Cultural Revolution were discontinued because of poor quality.[32] In 1985 the figure was 48,614,400.[33] World Bank projections are for steady growth to 70,000,000 by the end of the century[34] as more and more emphasis is put on the modernization policy's need for middle level technical and managerial skills.

For all the criticism of the Cultural Revolution for the damage it did to education, the animus must be directed at a decline in quality, not numbers of students exposed to schooling. The dramatic decline in elementary school enrollment since 1976, and particularly in the early 1980s is due to introduction of the "responsibility system" in the countryside and increased potential for making money in "sideline" occupations. As the family has again become the basic economic unit, children, especially females, have been put to work. The school drop-out rate is very high especially in the first grade. It was estimated in 1983 that only about 65% would complete grade five.[35] This figure casts doubt on the Chinese claim of an 80% literacy rate, especially since enrollment in adult spare-time elementary education declined from 21 million in 1979 to 8 million in 1983.[36] It will take a considerable amount of publicity and other persuasion to convince peasants that education of their children will increase their well-being, especially when many rural schools have been so obviously inadequate.

In cities, where the new economic policies do not provide an inducement to quit school and go to work, the one-child population policy, which has had much more impact on urban than rural areas, has already had an impact on enrollment and that will continue.

The enrollment decline, then, strongly suggests that the major effort to improve teaching should be directed at in-service training, and at better utilization of the teachers of highest quality. Teachers in China generally have a light teaching load compared to teachers elsewhere. During the years of enrollment decline the teaching staff increased slightly, making the student/teacher ratio in elementary schools decline from 27:1 in 1979 to 23:1 in 1983. The median ratio for other LDC's is about 35:1. The declining ratio has not led to smaller class size, which remains at an average of about 34 students, but rather to reduced teaching loads, which average 10–12 periods per week. A common load in economically advanced countries is 20–25 periods per week. World Bank analysts argue that higher work loads with fewer but better qualified teachers could improve the quality of education while reducing the cost. The savings could be used for better salaries and equipment.[37]

Secondary Education: Structural Reorganization with Emphasis on Development of Vocational and Technical Education

Technical and vocational training is the weakest link in China's system of education, and a major deterrent to the realization of economic goals, according to the "Decision on Education Reform."[38] The percentage of the total Chinese labor force classified as technicians is only about 1.3%, including teachers, health workers and others. In the agricultural sector the figure is 0.1%. In industry, estimates vary from 2.8% to 5%. The average in other countries, both developing and advanced, is 8.7%.[39]

A lack of middle-level technicians is particularly acute. The rates of middle-level to university trained technicians in China is about 1:1.[40] In some critical industries it is much lower. For instance, in the Capital Iron and Steel Company it is 1:10; in the Shanghai metallurgical industry it is 1:7.[41] A more appropriate ratio, according to World Bank analysts, would be 3:1.[42] The scarcity of middle-level technicians and skilled workers means that many middle-level jobs such as supervisor, designer, laboratory technician, agrarian technician, skilled machinery operator, and so on, are filled either by underqualified workers, or overqualified university graduates. The latter situation, implicit in the ratios cited above, is explicit in a recent survey of twenty cities and provinces which revealed that 19% of the 1981 and 1982 university graduates in engineering had been assigned to jobs not commensurate with their training.[43]

The Chinese attribute the problem to "an irrationally structured secondary education system"[44] in which the overwhelming majority of secondary school students receive a general education in regular secondary schools, and graduate with no particular skills. Only a very small percentage go on to institutions of higher education; the rest must enter the work force. In 1984 there were 38.6 million students in regular junior secondary schools (grades 7–9) and 6.9 million in regular senior secondary schools (grades 10–12). By comparison, only 1.3 million were in secondary vocational schools, and 639,000 in secondary technical schools.[45] Total university and college enrollment, including that of two year colleges, was only about 1.5 million in 1984.

The current plan is to convert many of the regular, senior secondary schools to vocational and technical schools, and to create new vocational and technical schools so that the ratio between them and regular senior secondary schools will be 1:1 within five years. An article in the *People's Daily* in January, 1986 indicates extraordinarily rapid progress toward that goal—the ratio was reported to be already 1:1.28.[46] (Unfortunately the article does not mention the student ratio which would be more disproportionate if enrollment in the regular schools is greater than in the specialized schools, which is probably the case.)[47]

The main factor cited in the "Decision" to account for the "irrational structure" of secondary education is the residual influence of the Cultural Revolution, during which time secondary education was restructured. In the late 1950s, 15–20% of secondary school students were in vocational and technical programs or institutions. By 1970 the figure was about 1%.[48] The attrition was due to the perception during the Cultural Revolution that a two-track education system was prejudicial to the goals of social transformation and equality. Cultural Revolution education policies stipulated that schools were to offer a single curriculum which combined academic study with physical labor. All schools were to be directly linked with production units and through them, offer practical training. What, in fact, happened in those years is that the politics of class struggle superceded all else, and little academic education or systematic, specialized training was accomplished. Renunciation of Cultural Revolution policies after 1976 resulted in a strong reassertion of the value of academic education. The curriculum reflected a primary concern with preparing students for university entrance examinations, even though university placement allocations excluded all but a select few. Specialized education was relatively neglected. With the publication of the "Decision on Education Reform" it has been receiving unprecedented attention.

The "Decision" outlines a number of measures to strengthen vocational and technical education. From now on, when production units hire employees, they must select first from the graduates of V and T schools. All applicants for jobs requiring special skills will be required to take competence tests and receive a certificate of fitness before being employed. That stipulation will gradually be extended to veteran employees as expanded opportunities for retraining on the job are developed. Graduates of regular junior secondary schools will be given short-term training before entering the labor market.[49]

Much of the burden for developing vocational and technical education is falling on local areas and on particular enterprises. Economic and political units of all sorts are exhorted to run specialized schools, either by themselves or in conjunction with local education offices. In addition to training their own employees, these units are encouraged to train those of other units, and to accept independent applicants who will pay their own fees.

To compensate for a serious deficiency of trained teachers, the units are advised to invite teachers from other units and from schools to "moonlight" for extra pay, and to direct scientific and technical personnel, skilled workers and master craftsmen to teach part-time. The emphasis is on innovation and diversity in the use of personnel, facilities, curriculum, and teaching methods.[50]

As in the case of elementary schools, it will probably be a long time before an adequate teaching staff is found to service the secondary schools. People with the requisite skills have numerous options for employment, and will generally find greater inducements, material and psychological, in professions other than teaching.

Another serious problem faces even those schools with adequate teaching staff, unless the past approach to vocational and technical education in China changes. Reflecting its origin in the Soviet system, vocational and technical education has been so narrowly specialized that the skills acquired can quickly become obsolete as China modernizes. The remedy is to make technical training more general and theoretical and add more general education courses to the curriculum. That seems to be the direction that specialized secondary school training is taking in China, but the issue has been little discussed in print.

Higher Education: Reforming the Management System, Enrollment Policies and Job Allocation Procedures

The key to reform at the highest level of the education system, according to the "Decision on Education Reform," is to do away with "excessive management" by government offices and grant more autonomy to the individual institutions of higher education. So long as they act in accordance with national policies, laws, and plans, colleges and universities will have unprecedented authority to manage their own affairs. That includes having the authority to hire and dismiss school officials at the vice-president level and below; to determine the specific usage of capital investment funds and other monies from the State; to raise money themselves; to adjust the direction of their specialized services, determine their own teaching plans and curriculum, and select and write their own teaching materials; to establish relationships with outside units, accepting research assignments from them, training their personnel, and cooperating in teaching, scientific research and production projects; and to develop, independently, international educational and scholarly exchanges. The new Education Commission reserves the prerogative to grant other authority to particular institutions depending on the circumstances.[51]

While relinquishing many of the direct bureaucratic controls that have characterized higher education administration heretofore, government education offices have been given increased oversight responsibility. Specifically, they have been told to form teams of educators, intellectuals and employers to assess management quality and reward the best schools with commendations and material benefits. Schools that are poorly run will be told to reform or cease operation.[52] What has happened, in effect, is the application to education of the "responsibility system" developed for economic institutions.

Experiments in the past several years with procedures for student enrollment and post-graduation job assignment have now been certified by the "Decision." Three methods are used. The first, enrollment and assignment by government plan, is a continuation of procedures in effect most of the time since 1949. Based on government forecast of labor needs, students are enrolled in particular educational institutions, taking into account their preferences and their scores on the national entrance examination. Special consideration is given to students from remote areas or students who pledge to work in those areas or at particularly rigorous and difficult jobs. There is also a preferential quota for students who will serve in the People's Liberation Army upon graduation.[53]

Job assignment of university graduates has been the responsibility of the State for many years. Almost all graduates have been placed in state-run enterprises in accordance with allocation procedures based on the state plan, student preference and requests by hiring units. Many graduates will continue to be so assigned, but an increasing number will make their own arrangements, or will be assigned on the basis of direct contacts between the schools and employers, without the mediation of central government offices. In the future it is possible that only the most critical occupations, including teaching, will be filled by state assignment.

There is a conjunction of reinforcing reasons for this change of job assignment procedure. Many graduates prefer more flexibility in the determination of their employment. Jobs with state enterprises and agencies, while secure, are no longer necessarily the most lucrative or interesting, given recent changes in the economic system. Educational institutions have been critical of the old system of guaranteed employment for graduates because of its negative, "iron rice bowl" effect on student motivation. And finally, employing units have wanted more leeway to determine their own needs and select their own employees. Individual enterprises not previously favored by the government can now compete for the best graduates; and, no longer must they accept everyone assigned to them.

The second method for enrollment and assignment is known as the "entrustment" (*weituo*) system, whereby particular units are entrusted with student selection. They arrange with education institutions to enroll some of their employees who have passed the national entrance examination. Upon graduation, or completion of a special training program, the students return to the sponsoring work unit. The units pay the schools, often in excess of the direct cost of education. "Profits" made by the schools are reinvested in education. The "Decision" stipulates that this method must be gradually expanded, "making it a major supplement to national admissions planning."[54] In 1983 there were 3000 such students. In 1985 there were 58,000.[55]

The third method allows for admission of a small number of self-financed students who have passed the national examination. They apply on their own, and are responsible for finding their own jobs after graduation, though they can ask the school for placement assistance if they wish. The number of such students is growing rapidly, with the encouragement of educational institutions which make a profit on tuition.

As the latter two enrollment methods suggest, the fee structure of university education is changing dramatically. In the past, all costs of higher education were borne by the state, including a stipend for needy students. State expenditures per university student, as a percentage of GNP, were the highest in the world, reversing the situation for primary and secondary education. The "Decision" calls for reforms whereby tuition and miscellaneous fees will be paid by the students, with exceptions for those in financial need, those training to be teachers, and those whose post-graduation jobs will be particularly difficult or in remote areas. Scholarships will be available for academic excellence. Students already in school will be financed according to the system in effect when they entered.[56]

Other trends in financing and in management innovation are apparent in recent practices in Jiaotong University in Shanghai.[57] Its controversial mode of operation, once the subject of vigorous debate, received commendation from Deng Xiaoping in 1984, and was subsequently publicized as a model for emulation. Taking full advantage of increased managerial autonomy, Jiaotong led the way in establishing outside research connections, with an emphasis on practical projects that would yield quick results and substantial profits. It used its new sources of income to improve faculty salaries and living conditions, hire new personnel, recruit outstanding students with scholarship inducements, and attract foreign scholars.

Critics contend that Jiaotong was sacrificing basic science research and instruction in the interest of monetary gain. Concern was also expressed by comprehensive universities with strong programs in the liberal arts and social sciences that did not have the same potential for financial gain as universities of engineering and science such as Jiaotong.[58] The support of the central leadership for the Jiaotong model does not resolve all of the substantive issues in the controversy surrounding it, but it does accelerate the trend toward managerial decentralization, and reinforce the impetus to innovate in all aspects of higher education.

The experience of Qinghua University provides another illustration of recent trends in higher education. Qinghua, an engineering and science university, like Jiaotong, has been encouraging its students to broaden their education with courses in history, culture, society and foreign languages. The Soviet model of narrow specialization in polytechnic institutions is being significantly modified. Rigorous requirements for degrees in particular disciplines have been relaxed and students are encouraged to take elective courses for the first time. Attendance in class is no longer compulsory and will not be a factor in assessing the student's grade as previously. Accelerated courses have been offered, enabling some students to graduate ahead of time or earn two degrees in different fields. Research, which until recently was not considered a major mission of the universities, but was largely the province of special research institutes, is now a major concern at Qinghua. In 1985 the university was engaged in some 500 research projects, many of them contracted for by production units for a fee. Another monetary inducement for research was passage of a patent law in April 1985, the first since the establishment of the PRC. Qinghua has already applied for 168 patents.

Although the great majority of Qinghua students pursue graduate studies (1200 of 1900 graduates in 1985), the university is a leader in job assignment experimentation. It was one of four national universities that did not rely on the central government at all to place its graduates. Most were placed by the university, the rest found employment on their own.[59]

Graduate training is a growing concern at Qinghua and other institutions of higher learning. All graduate programs were discontinued in 1966 with the onset of the Cultural Revolution. In 1977 they were reinstated. The first students were enrolled in 1978. In 1980 advanced degrees were reintroduced for the first time since the Anti-rightist Campaign in 1957. By 1984, 22 of China's approximately 900 institutions of higher learning were allowed to form graduate faculties, and 1,143 of 247,000 university faculty members were certified to supervise doctoral students. In 1982, 16,000 master's degrees were awarded and five doctorates. Fifteen more doctorates were awarded in 1983.[60] A *People's Daily* article notes that there were 46,500 graduate students in China in 1984. That number is supplemented by some 20,000 Chinese students, mostly graduate students, who have studied abroad since 1979.[61]

With the growth of graduate studies, attention is being directed toward post-doctoral studies. An article in *People's Daily* reported that in 1985,

250 students were enrolled in special post-doctoral research centers in 73 universities and research institutes.[62]

Perhaps the greatest departure from the past in higher education is the recent proliferation of different kinds of institutions, many of them experimental. More often than not, they are under local control. Some are affiliated with foreign institutions.

The most rapidly growing new style institution is the non-residential community college. Before 1980, all higher education was residential. By the end of 1985, non-residential colleges enrolled 75,000 students.[63] Training at these institutions is mostly vocational and technical, emphasizing skills in such occupations as secretarial work, library work, accounting, statistics, law, electronics, computer science, management, and so on. Courses generally run from one to three years.

Non-residential colleges are a comparatively inexpensive way of providing higher level training. All of the students pay tuition and fees. All find their own employment after graduation, or through direct negotiations between the college and employers. The State plays no role. Supplemental funding is usually provided by local governments, but alternative sources are solicited. The World Bank, for instance, has provided loans for seventeen such schools.[64]

One community college, Jianghan College in Wuhan, has established mutually beneficial relations with a community college in Ohio.Such foreign contact, considered an unthinkable anathema a few years ago, is becoming increasingly common. A notable example is the China National Training Center for Industrial Scientific and Technical Management in Dalian. Established in 1980 in accordance with a Sino-U.S. Agreement on Scientific and Technological cooperation, it is managed jointly by the U.S. Department of Commerce and the Chinese State Commissions for Science and Technology and for Economics. The two governments share the funding, and cooperate in determining the curriculum. Courses are taught by staff from each country. Between 1980 and 1985, 76 U.S. professors and specialists have taught at the Center. Programs include six month seminars for high level state officials, factory managers, university administrators, and so on, and a two year enterprise management course in cooperation with the State University of New York at Buffalo. In addition, an MBA degree is granted to advanced students who complete the required courses at the SUNY Buffalo campus and participate in a work-study internship with a U.S. corporation.[65]

Another example of foreign influence in Chinese higher education is Yellow River University (Huang He Daxue) in Zhengzhou, Henan Province. It is an explicitly U.S. style institution founded and directed by an American citizen of Chinese descent. Students take a broad spectrum of courses in the arts and sciences, as well as in specialized fields.

Initital funding was solicitied mainly from Chinese Americans. Henan provincial officials provided facilities, including a 300 acre campus that was once a retreat for the top leadership of the Communist Party, plus maintenance staff and supplemental funding for faculty and students. Students all pay tuition and fees. Much of the faculty is American. Courses are generally taught in English. In 1985 there were approximately three hundred students, more than half of them at the graduate level. Enrollment plans call for 5,000 students within five years, and 10,000 within ten years.[66]

Alternative Education

Supplementing the regular school system is a variety of alternative higher education opportunities. They are classified in six categories by the Chinese—evening universities, correspondence colleges, radio and television universities, workers' colleges, spare-time colleges, and independent study with a qualifying examination.

Evening universities are run by regular universities. Classes are taught by university faculty for extra pay. Students take twelve hours of classes a week and earn a two year college certificate in three years, or a regular diploma in five years. In 1984 there were 140 evening universities with 50,000 students.[67]

Correspondence colleges are similar in every respect except they cater mainly to students who live too far from campus to attend classes regularly. Ten institutions were offering correspondence courses to about 200,000 students in 1984.[68]

Radio and Television Universities have an enrollment almost equal to that of regular institutions of higher learning. In 1985, 1.4 million students were enrolled in degree programs. There are 20,000 classes throughout the country for students who wish to study together rather than independently. 150 courses are offered in 100 specialties by over 10,000 full-time teachers and 20,000 part-time teachers. From 1983–1985, 300,000 students earned degrees, and another 400,000 earned certificates in a specialty. In 1986 the State will have a special channel for educational TV for the first time. Also for the first time, recent high school graduates, and not just workers and others who have been out of school for several years, will be allowed to sit for entrance examinations.[69]

Worker's spare-time colleges are usually run by a city, a city district, or an administrative department. They register with the Education Commission, are examined by higher authorities, and certified to grant degrees. There are over 800 such colleges offering courses in arts and sciences and specialized fields such as languages, architecture, law and production skills—particularly those suited to local needs.[70]

All four of the alternative higher education programs mentioned above are open only to those who pass entrance examinations. In late 1985 the Education Commisssion decided to create a unified entrance examination for all in an effort to control and improve quality.[71]

Spare-time colleges, as the name implies, are for those with regular jobs who wish to improve their skills or develop new ones. They are run by institutions of all sorts and serve millions of people. For instance, in the past five years, over 5 million administrative cadres have attended spare-time classes in fundamental knowledge of economics and administration. Spare-time classes at the higher level supplement those at lower levels. By 1985 over 30 million workers had attended spare-time education classes offered in the past several years.[72]

Independent study with qualifying examinations for certificates and degrees is being pursued by an increasing number of people in China. Qualifying examinations were introduced in Beijing City in 1984. To support the program, the Municipal Personnel Department stipulated that employers should elevate people to positions commensurate with their learning when they passed qualifying examinations. Those without jobs would be recommended to employers by the examination committee. Most provinces, municipalities and autonomous regions have followed the Beijing model and have administered examinations to hundreds of thousands of people.[73]

The most recent innovation in "higher" education is the creation in several large cities of 61 new "universities" for retired older people. They offer courses in health, psychology, literature, cooking, gardening, photography and so on. Over 30,000 people were reported to be attending in 1985 and the number is expected to grow rapidly.[74]

Problems and Prospects

In assessing the prospects for fulfilling the three areas of special concern articulated by the 1985 "Decision on Education Reform," three problems seem particularly salient.

The first is the problem of maintaining a momentum for educational growth and reform in local areas, and among work units, as they are obliged to assume increasing responsibility for finance and management. Devolution of responsibility poses virtually no problem for institutions of higher education. They will continue to be heavily financed by the state and will have new opportunities to increase their income from other sources; and, they can only welcome less government interference into management of their affairs. The problem becomes apparent at the secondary level and increases substantially at the elementary level. Work units and villages are being asked, in effect, to reallocate human and material resources, benefitting education at the expense of other concerns. The positive material effects of this will be long-term, whereas the negative effects, for those who lose in the reallocation process, are immediate. There could be considerable resistance. The government has provided little but exhortation, so far, to induce significant reallocation. If past experience is any guide, change will not come rapidly unless more than words provide the impetus.

The second problem is related to the first: How will educational institutions attract sufficiently well-trained personnel to fulfill their mission? Again the problem increases at successively lower levels. For all that is being done now to increase the material well-being, status and respect for teachers, most people with adequate education and skills have opportunities to assume other positions where their talents are also desperately needed. The state may have to do more than it has already done to make teaching sufficiently appealing to attract well-qualified personnel.

The third problem, that of equity and equality, goes to the heart of the continuing debate in China over the meaning of socialism, and the methods to achieve it. During the Cultural Revolution, the policy, if not the practice, was to "build on the least"—to give advantages to those who, formerly, were most deprived. The strategy today for realizing the "four modernizations" is to "build on the best." That is, to build on strength; to allocate resources where the immediate impact will be greatest. The "key" school and rigorous entrance examinations are manifestations of that policy, as is the increasing devolution of financial responsibility. The prospects for students from relatively privileged homes are improved, as are those for urban areas in contrast to rural areas, and for rich rural areas in contrast to poorer areas. The government is making some efforts to aid the poorest areas through fiscal policies, special allocations and exhortations, but the prospect for increased disparity, at least for the short term, is likely. The current reasoning is that everyone will eventually benefit if "some get rich first." "Trickle-down" is seen as preferable to what is regarded as the only alternative—an equality of poverty. If critics question the plausibility of trickle-down, they are not currently being heard. Increasing disparity is the price the current socialist leadership seems to be willing to pay for rapid economic growth. Whether that is a long-term or short-term prospect remains to be seen.

Meanwhile, more people are enrolled in education programs in China than in any other country in the world. A *People's Daily* report in January 1986 states that over 100 million people, about 10% of the total population, are engaged in formal study of some sort.[75] That is an impressive accomplishment for any society. But for one in which 60% of the total population is below the age of twenty-five, there is still room for improvement.

Notes

1. *Renmin Ribao* (People's Daily), Overseas edition (hereafter *RMRB*), September 26, 1985.
2. *Beijing Review* (hereafter, *BR*), August 19, 1985, p.6.
3. *BR*, December 16, 1985, p.15. See *Ten Percent Sample of China Population Census*, (Beijing: State Statistical Bureau, 1983.)
4. *BR*, December 15, 1985, p.16.
5. *China: Long Term Development Issues and Options. A World Bank Country Economic Report*, (Baltimore: Johns Hopkins Press for the World Bank, 1985), p.124.
6. *China: Issues and Prospects in Education*. Washington, D.C.: The World Bank, 1985 (hereafter, *CIPE*), pp.6–7. *RMRB*, January 27, 1986 says 95.9% of school age children are now enrolled in elementary school. That figure is a rough estimate and gives no indication of the drop-out rate.
7. *CIPE*, p.70.
8. *China Reconstructs*, (hereafter *CR*), November, 1985, p.15.
9. *CIPE*, p.ix.
10. The "Decision" is published in *RMRB*, May 29, 1985, and in *Guanyu jiaoyu tizhi gaige de wenjian* (Documents on reform of the education system), (Beijing: Renmin chuban she, 1985.) (hereafter, *Jiaoyu wenjian*), pp. 1–18.
11. Deng's speech is in *Jiaoyu wenjian*, pp.44–46.
12. "Decision," *Jiaoyu wenjian*, pp.1–18.
13. *Ibid.*, p.7.
14. *BR*, March 18, 1985, and *RMRB*, November 22, 1985, have articles on China's first schools for the mentally handicapped, established in Beijing, September, 1984.
15. *BR*, December 23, 1985, p.20.
16. *CIPE*, pp.10–11.
17. *Ibid.*, p.45. *BR*, December 30, 1985, p.23 says that between 1950–1983 the state spent 6.6% of its budget on education. *CIPE* refers to both state and non-state funds, e.g., those generated by collectives and other sources.
18. *BR*, September 9, 1985, p.4.
19. *BR*, September 2, 1985, p.8.
20. *Ibid.*
21. *Ibid.*, p.9.
22. *RMRB*, June 22, 1985.
23. *BR*, September 2, 1985, p.9.
24. *BR*, December 30, 1985, p.23.
25. *Ibid.*
26. *RMRB*, December 11, 1985. *BR*, September 9, 1985, p.4.

27. *China Daily*, overseas edition, (hereafter *CD*), November 11, 1985.
28. *CIPE*, p.36.
29. *RMRB*, December 29, 1985. See also, *CD*, November 22, 1985.
30. *CIPE*, p.70.
31. *Ibid.*, pp.70–71. Wang Juefei, a research associate at the Beijing Teachers' University, argues that those figures do not take sufficient account of the population now at prime reproduction age and therefore the need for teachers is greater than the World Bank analysts suppose.
32. *CIPE*, pp.70–71.
33. *BR*, December 30, 1985, p.22.
34. *CIPE*, p.71.
35. *Ibid.*, p.8.
36. *Ibid.*, p.67.
37. *Ibid.*, p.9.
38. *Jiaoyu wenjian*, p.8.
39. *CIPE*, p.24.
40. *Ibid.*
41. *BR*, December 16, 1985, p.17.
42. *CIPE*, p.24.
43. *CR*, November 1985, p.17.
44. *Jiaoyu wenjian*, p.10.
45. *CR*, November, 1985, p.17.
46. *RMRB*, January 27, 1986.
47. *BR*, September 16, 1985 gives the figure 1,537,000 in secondary technical schools, or a ratio of 1:4.5 using the 1984 enrollment figure of 6.9 million students.
48. *CIPE*, p.25.
49. *Jiaoyu wenjian*, p.9.
50. *Ibid.*, pp.8–11.
51. *Jiaoyu wenjian*, p.13.
52. *Ibid.*
53. *Ibid.*, p.11.
54. *Ibid.*, p.12.
55. *BR*, December 30, 1985, p.23.
56. *Jiaoyu wenjian*, p.12.
57. Stanley Rosen, ed., "Higher Education Reform in the People's Republic of China," *Chinese Education*, Winter 1985–86, pp.3–33.
58. *Ibid.*, p.5.
59. *CR*, November, 1985, pp.18–24.
60. Julia Kwong, ed., "Graduate Programs in the People's Republic of China," *Chinese Education*, Fall 1985, pp.1–10 ff.
61. *RMRB*, January 31, 1986.
62. *RMRB*, November 24, 1986.
63. *CD*, December 4, 1985.
64. *Ibid.*
65. *BR*, December 30, 1985, pp.18–20.

66. *Liaowang Zhoukan* (Outlook Weekly) overseas edition, February 3, 1986, pp.34–35.
67. *BR*, August 6, 1984, p.26.
68. *Ibid.*, p.27.
69. *RMRB*, January 13, 1986.
70. *BR*, August 6, 1984, p.27.
71. *RMRB*, December 18, 1985.
72. *RMRB*, December 31, 1985.
73. *BR*, August 6, 1984, p.28.
74. *CD*, December 6, 1985. *RMRB*, February 4, 1986.
75. *RMRB*, January 27, 1986.

6
New Directions in Chinese Science and Technology

Richard P. Suttmeier

In March 1985, the Chinese Communist Party Central Committee announced a decision to reform the nation's science and technology system. This was but the latest of a series of important policy developments directed towards science and technology (S&T) in the post-Mao era. The March decision is usefully seen against a background of changes going back to the late 1970s.

The Chinese faced many problems with S&T following the Cultural Revolution decade (1966–76). The initial attack on these problems focused on reorganization to restore the system which existed before the Cultural Revolution, on raising the status of technical intellectuals who had suffered discrimination and at times humiliation during the Cultural Revolution, and on a grandiose program of scientific and technological development which stressed basic research and "Big Science," and the importation of foreign technology in the form of whole plants and equipment.

By the early 1980s, a consensus had been reached that this initial post-Mao program for revitalizing S&T was not a realistic response to Chinese conditions. It was too expensive, and it postulated a set of research priorities which did not have sufficient promise for meeting the needs of the economy. Thus in the period from 1980–82, emphasis shifted to the importance of applications. The slogan "science and technology should support the economy, and economic development must depend on science and technology" became the order of the day.

Apart from this new emphasis on the relationships between research and production, something more happened to science policy thinking in this period. The Chinese began to reflect upon the virtues and limitations of the pre-Cultural Revolution system, a system which had just been reaffirmed in 1978. The strength of the pre-Cultural Revolution system had been its contributions to the development of strategic national defense technologies, but its weakness was precisely in its limited ability to contribute to economic development. In light of these considerations, the strategy for the modernization of S&T since 1983 has combined the setting of goals for research and technology acquisition with a major commitment to reform the system.

Science and Technology in China's Future

In considering the reforms, it is helpful to first examine Chinese expectations for the future of S&T. In keeping with the emphasis on applications, Chinese policy thinking has come to stress the primacy of technological objectives, rather than the primacy of scientific research opportunities. Thus "technology policy" has superseded "science policy." The elements of this technology policy include the following:

First, the technologies needed to modernize China's infrastructure will be stressed. These include the many different types of technologies required in the energy, transportation and telecommunications industries.

Second, there is a great need for China to upgrade, or transform, the technologies in its established traditional industries and this has assumed major importance in China's array of priorities. Indeed, a special, well funded program for this purpose has been established and is being run by the State Economic Commission. One prominent example of what the Chinese believe needs to be done is the incorporation of modern electronic control technologies into the manufacturing and processing industries. This is part of a more general objective of having the world's "advanced" technologies of the 1970s and 1980s widely disseminated and used throughout the Chinese economy by the year 2000.

At the same time, the Chinese have become convinced that there is a "new technological revolution" going on in the world in the form of emerging science based industries. These are perceived as the future basis for national wealth and power, and the Chinese do not want to reach the end of the century still 20–30 years behind the more advanced nations in these fields. Thus, in addition to the popularization of the technologies of the 70s and 80s for the economy generally, for selected areas of high technology—microelectronics and computers, biotechnology, materials, robotics, new materials, optical fibers, and the technologies of ocean exploitation—the Chinese hope to reach parity with the advanced nations by the year 2000.

The challenge for the Chinese in meeting these objectives is to find the right mix of indigenous research and development and of foreign technology to be transferred into China. Foreign technology will be important for the technological transformation of traditional industries, and will play a role in the high-technology industries as well. But the Chinese realize that for the latter, they must by the end of the century have their own indigenous capability. To the extent that there will be contributions from abroad for this task, perhaps the most important is, and will continue to be, the advanced training of Chinese students in the sciences.

However, the more basic need is to achieve the linkages between research and production which have been so weak in the past. At China's better research institutes, there is often a sound *scientific* understanding of the state of the art in these new high technology industries, and the potential for research programs that would provide the scientific basis for the year 2000 goals. The infusion of bright young people with advanced training at the world's leading research centers will add to this capability. The conversion of scientific understanding into new industries, however, requires major changes in the ways both the economy and the S&T system are organized and operated. Hence, the programs of reform.

Why Reform?

What is to be reformed? The problem of the separation of research from production has its origins in the 1950s, and is very much a function of China's decision to emulate the Soviet approach to the organization of S&T at that time. The main features of the "Soviet model" are (1) its centralized research academies (including a national academy of sciences, and industrial research centralized in a few academies or institutes, serving the needs of an entire industry), (2) centralized research planning, (3) centralized resource allocation in the form of annual appropriations to research institutes, (4) high priority accorded to a military research and development (R&D) system which is largely isolated from the civilian economy and research system, and (5) a deemphasis of research in institutions of higher education.

Underlying these organizational arrangements has been the assumption that technological innovation is driven by, and will flow naturally out of the results of R&D. In addition, an article of faith in the Soviet model is that technical knowledge in a socialist society belongs to the whole people. It is a free public good which is not bought and sold. This ideological orientation has had the effect in China of undervaluing such knowledge, and of removing incentives for its production and utilization.

By the late 1970s, these assumptions and organizational arrangements had been modified and corrupted by the Cultural Revolution. The assumption of strong central direction, for instance, was compromised by the disruption of central planning mechanisms during the 1966–76 decade. Instead, power over research was concentrated in the various "systems" (*xitong*), such as the Academy of Sciences and the ministries, without any effective superordinate coordination and policy making. China was left with a series of vertically oriented bureaucracies for research and production, with little horizontal interchange. It had the worst of the Soviet model without what are, in theory, its benefits.

Other problems facing the Chinese system, which it is hoped the reforms will solve, include serious misallocations of technical manpower and of material resources for research. Problems of inefficiencies and duplications within the R&D system are also targeted. These problems, again, are a function of the organization of the system, and the Cultural Revolution years. As noted above, during this period, the planning and centralized administrative systems required to make the Soviet model work were disrupted. A consequence of this breakdown was an increase in the power of the ministries, as we have seen, but also in the discretionary power of the leading cadres of China's institutes and factories (what the Chinese call the *danwei*, or work unit). Under the conditions of the Cultural Revolution, these leaders were able to carve out power bases or "independent kingdoms" for themselves. They were thus able to resist central policy directives and to avoid the wider needs of the society, particularly with regard to the proper utilization of technical personnel.

The Reform Program

The main elements of the reform program, including changes which preceded the March 1985 decision mentioned at the outset, include the following:

1. *Centralization and decentralization.* The current reforms can usefully be seen first as part of a larger political agenda to overcome what many regard as the pathologies in the body politic which developed during the Cultural Revolution. In particular, for the other objectives of the S&T reforms to be realized, there is a need to undercut the discretionary powers of the ministerial systems of *xitong* and the work unit or *danwei*. Thus discernible in the reforms is a simultaneous centralization and decentralization having this objective.

Since the early 1980s, the Chinese have tried to increase the power of the central authorities over science policy. The most notable manifestations of these efforts have been the strengthening of the science policy role of the State Science and Technology Commission (SSTC), the expanded role in S&T policy of the State Economic and Planning Commissions, and the establishment, in 1983, of the Science and

Technology Leading Group as a supra-ministerial policy and coordinating body.

At the same time, the reform program of March 1985 ratifies and legitimizes a drift in the other direction towards greater autonomy for research institutes. While more autonomous (thus more cut off from ministerial patronage and protection), they must also face increasing competitive pressures from the "technology markets" described below. Simultaneous centralization and decentralization are not necessarily contradictory, however, if they are understood as efforts to erode the power of centralized ministries over S&T.

2. *Funding.* Apart from the fact that the amount of money being spent on R&D seems to be going up, one of the most significant measures of the reform program is to alter the established mechanisms for funding. The objective here is to break from the idea of block funding of institutes through annual appropriations, a hallmark of the Soviet mode. In China, this approach to funding had led to institute expectations of support from the state as a matter of entitlement, the "iron rice bowl" and "eating from the same big pot" phenomena which have afflicted the economy as a whole.

The two main reforms in funding research are the establishment of national science "funds" which are dispensed through a competitive peer review process, and the widespread adoption of contract research practices (and the gradual discontinuation of central state funding in many cases). The science fund idea, which has now been further institutionalized with the formal establishment in February, 1986 of the Chinese Science Foundation (CSF), is intended mainly for the support of basic research. The most prominent of the science funds prior to the establishment of the new CSF had been the one administered by the Chinese Academy of Sciences (CAS), which was established in 1982 on a trial basis, and which had been allocating about 70% of its funds to universities. With the reduction of block grant funding within the CAS, it is likely that there will be increasing competition between the Academy and the universities for CSF support. In anticipation of this, the budget for the Foundation is to grow more rapidly than the overall science budget during the next few years. There is some evidence, however, that some of the scientists in the CAS are uncomfortable with the CSF idea since it will make funding less predictable, and will tend to centralize support for basic research to a single source.

The reform in contract research, intended to apply more to the areas of applied research and development, takes two forms. The first is the encouragement of contractual arrangements for research between research institutes and enterprises, and the simultaneous reduction of the budgets of the former. As a rough approximation, some 30% of the funding for institutes engaged in applied R&D now comes from contracts, and the Chinese expect that percentage to increase as the funding formula changes are gradually implemented over the next five years.

The contract research approach is also being used for the procurement of research services for the priority areas of the state's plans. There are some 80 such areas in the next (seventh) five year plan. Contrary to past practices when these projects were centrally assigned, now bids for the projects will be solicited, and research institutes which choose to bid will compete with each other for the contract. This emergence of research contracting has the intent of changing the economic and administrative status of many research institutes, particularly those previously "free standing" institutes under the central ministries, and some of the institutes under the Academy of Sciences. There is some evidence that change has occurred. In the face of a decline in their centrally allocated budgets, some research institutes have been converted into economic enterprises, some have entered into joint ventures with production units, and some have merged with or have been absorbed by enterprises.

3. *Manpower Related Reforms.* Efforts have been made to permit a freer movement of technical personnel from job to job, either on a temporary basis, or permanently. According to recent surveys taken in fourteen provinces by the Chinese, the rate of mobility is terribly low. In 1983, only 2% of the technical work force experienced any mobility; the figure only rose to 3% in 1984.

There are three reasons why increased labor mobility is essential if China is to realize its expectations for S&T. First, there are still problems of individuals assigned to work for which they are unsuited and don't like, a situation which erodes morale. Second, technical manpower is concentrated in the free standing "independent" institutes which have no organic connection with industry, while industrial enterprises are often starved for technical talent. The reforms in funding noted above are intended to reduce the significance of the free standing institutes, but without reforms in labor allocation as well, the former will have only limited success.

Finally, the Chinese have come to realize that the goals they have for the diffusion of ideas and technology, and the linking of technical understanding with economic opportunities to form new high technology industries will be much more difficult to achieve in the absence of the movement of people. However, the kind of personnel mobility required is inconsistent with the tradition of tight political control over personnel matters which has been one of the most characteristic features of Communist rule in China. Thus, reform of the personnel allocation system is one of the most politically sensitive of the reforms. Nevertheless, some progress has been made.

New graduates, for instance, are to be given more voice in their initial assignments, and students returning from overseas study are to have their job preferences considered seriously. A labor market for technical personnel is being tried out on a limited basis, and there are a variety of new mechanisms ranging from specialized personnel exchange newsletters to what are in effect employment agencies for scientists and engineers.

As noted at the beginning of this section, the number of technical personnel who enjoy mobility opportunities is still very limited, and resistance to reform in the personnel system is deeply entrenched. For these reasons, the greatest hope for more flexibility in the utilization of scientists and engineers may lie in the more diffuse, overall marketization of the R&D system. Contract research, the rise of technical consulting services, and "moonlighting" opportunities for technical personnel may thus lead to more actual movement of talent than the formal reforms in the personnel system.[1]

4. *The Establishment of "Technology Markets."* This reform is related to the growth of contract research, but it goes beyond the latter. The establishment of technology markets represents in the first instance an ideological reform in which the economic status of technical knowledge has been redefined. Instead of being a free public good, it is now regarded as a commodity. As such, it can be bought and sold through market transactions. In some cases, technology markets have been specially organized ("technology fairs"); the technology market idea is part of the "marketization" of the economy more generally deriving from the economic reform policies.

The opening of technology markets inevitably brings with it questions of the pricing of technology, a problem with which the Chinese are now struggling. This problem—difficult in any economy—is made more so by the irrationalities of prices in the economy more generally. It also makes the question of intellectual property—who owns knowledge and what rights attend to owners—inescapable. The introduction of the new patent system in 1985 signals new approaches to these questions. By assigning, and presumably protecting, intellectual property rights, the patent system should clarify the respective positions of the sellers and buyers of technology in the market. It should also create new incentives for the producers of technology to become more innovative, and make consumers more sensitive to the economic value of the technology they procure.

5. *Reforms in Higher Education.* There are a number of reforms in this area having to do with the management and internal operations of

universities. Of particular note for our concerns here are changes which are allowing the universities to emerge as important research performers, thus breaking with the legacy of the Soviet model.

The institutionalization of a research tradition in China's universities will take time. The state had long starved the universities of research funds, and thus long before the current reforms, institutions of higher education have had to seek research funding from contracts or other relationships with industry. More often than not however, this has led to activities more aptly described as technical service, or industrial extension, rather than research.

With the initiation of Ph.D. programs, however, this heavy reliance on industrial funding will have to give way to new approaches to funding research of a more basic character. The use of the science funds has helped, and there is a newly established budget line from the State Education Commission to support institutional expenses incurred by Ph.D. granting institutions. Nevertheless, the strong emphasis placed on applications in national science policy and continuing funding problems, keeps pressure on the universities to maintain and expand relations with industry. In the view of some observers both in China and abroad, there is a danger in this of aborting the promise of a reformed higher education system, and harming the development of science over the long term.

Excessive attention to applications, it is feared, will attenuate the development of a basic research tradition in the universities, and with it the capability to train students with research competence. In addition, the pursuit of contract research and revenues for technical services by university faculties carries the danger that teaching will be neglected. These possibilities for distorting the role of the universities are made more pressing by the fact that often, the types of applied problems which the universities are asked to address are often scientifically mundane.

6. The Military Research and Production Systems. As part of the efforts to achieve better utilization of existing human and material resources, and as a reflection of the lower investment priority of the military, military facilities have been directed to turn their often considerable abilities to the service of the civilian economy. These changes are evident in activities ranging from the redirection of the Chinese nuclear and space programs, to the provision of discrete technical services by individual research institutes or factories under the military.

The "civilianization" of the military research and production system is an area of reform about which there is still considerable ignorance outside of China. Foreigner observers have thought that over the years the military has had a priority claim on human and material resources. This has allowed China to make the impressive achievements it has in nuclear weaponry, rocketry and space. Although the military reportedly received 50% of the 10 billion *yuan* 1985 national R&D budget, it also appears that the injunction to serve the civilian economy is being backed up by reductions in centrally allocated funds for many units in the military-industrial-research complex. Faced with the prospect of reduced budgets and with opportunities for profit in the civilian economy, there clearly are incentives for a degree of civilianization. On the other hand, reports from China indicate that not all units feel comfortable with this change, and visits to military facilities by foreigners often reveal that many of these are slow to change.

These visits have also revealed that the military industries have many of the problems of production which plague the civilian sector, especially the problem of bringing innovations into efficient serial production. In light of this, the effects of civilianization may not be all that is hoped for. Instead of aiding civilian R&D and production, this reform may complicate the job of improving the civilian sector. In addition, the military research and industry complex has had relatively comfortable existence, and there have been reports of considerable resistance within it to reforms which would make it more economically accountable.

The promise of this reform should not be underestimated however. A more effective linkage of the civilian and military systems could inject considerable technical expertise into the former, and by making the military also face market competition, the reform could lead to a far more efficient military industry in its service to both the civilian and military economies. It is the latter point which the reformers attempt to make to those who resist civilianization on the grounds that it will compromise China's national defense.

7. *The Diffusion of Technical Capabilities.* A strong theme in current S&T policies has been the encouragement of the growth of S&T capabilities in small cities and in rural areas. In some cases, the initiative for acquiring such capabilities has come from the smaller cities such as Changzhou and Shashi.

However, the central authorities have also been active in this area as well. The State Science and Technology Commission, for instance, recently announced a new policy (the "Spark Plan") to stimulate more advanced forms of technological innovation in the rural areas as part of a long term strategy of rural transformation. In addition, the Academy of Sciences has established new outreach programs to provinces and localities for the provision of research and technical services.

The Challenges Ahead

China's domestic science reform program is occurring in the midst of what for post-1949 China is an unprecedented interaction with world science and technology. Intergovernmental agreements for scientific cooperation have been signed with a score of advanced industrial countries, while Chinese universities and research institutes also maintain their own international agreements. Tens of thousands of Chinese scientists and science students have been or are abroad for training, international organizations have been assisting China in developing its infrastructure for science and technology, and China is in regular contact with high techonlogy firms negotiating for the transfer of technology.

These contacts are clearly a spur to the modernization of China's S&T, and provide reinforcement for the reform program. Whether China takes full advantage of the opportunities offered by these contacts, and whether they will have a sustained positive impact on Chinese modernization is of course up to the Chinese themselves.

China's leaders face many challenges in seeing the reform program through to its completion, not least of which is the challenge of managing the conflicts which the current course will inevitably produce. As noted above, the logic of the reforms is to effect a major system transformation, and any change so ambitious will surely produce resistance. The resistance will not be confined solely to the diehard Maoists or backers of the Soviet model, as is commonly assumed. Many scientists and engineers can also be expected to oppose parts of the reform program.

It is likely that the lines will be drawn in connection with five issues:

1. *Basic Research.* This is an area where some members of the scientific community are likely to oppose the reform leaders. How much basic research should be done—engaging how many people, and requiring how much investment—and how it should be supported, are questions which do not admit of easy answers in any country. The current emphasis on application has been challenged by some scientists as being a throwback to some of the darker days of Chinese science such as the Cultural Revolution or the Great Leap Forward years. While this complaint may be a bit of an overstatement, there clearly is a danger that a policy stressing applications, and the new approaches to funding, could in their implementation be insensitive to the importance of basic research for the long term good of China's science.

2. *The Future of the Academy.* Related to the issue of basic research is the question of the future of the Chinese Academy of Sciences. CAS is a large and cumbersome organization with nearly 120 research institutes and approximately 40,000 research personnel. While many of its scientists see it as the nation's center of basic research, in fact less than 20% of

its work is in basic science. If the Academy is more of an applied research and development organization, then its organizational separation as an autonomous agency from production enterprises is of questionable value.

The Chinese are therefore now wrestling with the question of the future of the CAS, and are trying to find a logic for its present form by studying the experiences of national laboratories in the U.S., French and German approaches to the organization of science. It is likely that during the next five years there will be many changes in the Academy, including the divestiture of many of its institutes. Such changes are unlikely to be made without controversy.

3. *Increasing Cosmopolitanism.* While the internationalizing of Chinese science holds many benefits as noted above, it also contains the seeds of conflict as well. Opposition from ideological conservatives has already been seen, and can be expected in the future. It is also possible to discern feelings of uneasiness among some scientists as well. Some of those who are Soviet trained may be less than enthusiastic about the strong tilt towards western ways of doing science now in course. Those unable to go abroad may envy those who are. Those more senior scientists responsible for the reintegration into the Chinese system of younger colleagues recently returned from abroad may find that the latter bring back with them unrealistic expectations about what can be accomplished in China. Finally, many Chinese scientists may harbor quiet resentments that foreign scientists seemingly have more of a voice with the Chinese government than they do. Students of modern Chinese history will recognize that issues of cosmopolitanism can be politically quite problematic.

4. *Personnel Mobility.* The opposition to reforms in this area is likely to come less from scientists than from more tradition-minded Party leaders and managerial cadres at all levels of the society. The former will fear that relaxation of the system of administrative allocations of personnel will threaten one of the Party's main instruments of power. The latter, who must always do their jobs in the face of uncertainties about the supply of necessary resources, will resist releasing personnel they control to market forces. Such resistance will continue to make implementation of reforms in this area go slowly. But the very slowness will threaten other parts of the reform program, and the reformers will thus push for more rapid changes in the personnel allocation system.

5. *Elitism.* The current direction of policy for science and education in China is clearly much more tolerant of the emergence of scientific elitism than was the case in the past. Chinese Communist society may in fact be more forgiving of elitism than is commonly assumed. However, elitism is of great symbolic importance, and can become problematic

under certain conditions. Should the scientific elite fail to perform up to the standards expected of it, conflicts in this area can be expected.

The question of elitism is ultimately linked with the issues of basic research and cosmopolitanism. If the scientific community is perceived to be drifting off into work which is designed to win the kudos of a foreign audience, but which offers few benefits to China, the symbolic power of allegations of elitism may once again be invoked as it has been in earlier periods of scientific development in the People's Republic, with such damaging results.

The likelihood of conflict over these or other issues by no means implies that current policies are inevitably doomed to failure. The policies are generally well conceived and are responsive to Chinese conditions. The various forms of international support China is now receiving also bodes well for the current course. But in implementing the new policies over the next five years, there will surely be conflicts over policy and resistance to implementation. The management of these conflicts will require skilled political leadership. China has had such leadership in the recent past, and there is reason to hope that it will have it in the near term future as well.

Notes

1. This point is made in an excellent paper by Leo A. Orleans on the reforms of the personnel system. Leo A. Orleans, "Reforms and Innovations in the Utilization of China's Scientific and Engineering Talent." Prepared for the Conference on "China's New Technological Revolution," Harvard University, May 9–11, 1986.

7
Taiwan in 1985: Quest for a Brighter Day

Parris H. Chang

For Taiwan, 1985 can be described as a year of political woes and financial scandals.

On January 16, the Government Information Office in Taipei announced that three top officials of the Intelligence Bureau of the Ministry of National Defense (IBMND), including the Bureau Director, Vice-Admiral Wong Hsi-ling[1] were involved in the murder of Henry Liu, an anti-government Chinese-American writer in Daly City, California, on October 15, 1984. Although it was three members of the "Bamboo Gang," the largest crime syndicate in Taiwan, who actually carried out the shooting, subsequent revelations showed that the order to "teach a lesson" to Henry Liu came from the Chief of the IBMND.

Although the Kuomintang (KMT or Chinese Nationalist) authorities initially denied any connection with Liu's death and banned or censored many local and foreign publications which suggested such linkage, they had to change their tack after the FBI reportedly acquired a tape recording in which the "Bamboo Gang" leader, Chen Chi-li, had supposedly named and implicated the high intelligence officials. On April 12, Admiral Wong and two other IBMND officials were put on trial in a military court, and one week later Wong was convicted and sentenced to life imprisonment while his two co-defendants each received two and a half year prison terms. Chen Chi-li and two of his gang members were also tried (one in absentia) for murder in Taipei District Court and were given life sentences in early April.

U.S. State Department spokesman Alan Romberg called the involvement of the Taiwan intelligence organization in the Liu murder "a very serious matter." A number of U.S. Senators and Congressmen, including some who used to be sympathetic to the KMT, were highly critical. They were particularly incensed when Taipei rejected U.S. requests for the gangsters' extradition. A hearing was held by the House Foreign Affairs Committee to determine whether the Liu murder was part of a "consistent pattern of acts of intimidation and harassment against individuals in the U.S." (A determination by the Congress along these lines would have implied the invocation of the Solarz Amendment, mandating the suspension of U.S. arms sales to Taiwan.)

In another incident, the Taiwan Garrison General Headquarters (TGGH), the organization responsible for Taiwan's internal security, arrested Ms. Lee Ya-ping, the publisher of a Los Angeles-based Chinese-language newspaper on September 17 on sedition charges. The paper, *The International Daily,* was accused of publishing pro-PRC articles and of distributing such materials inside Taiwan. The State Department lodged a strong protest and demanded her immediate release, in a stern statement that contained the Reagan administration's strongest criticism of the KMT authorities. Much to its embarrassment, the ROC government yielded within ten days with a face-saving formula and allowed Ms. Lee to return to the U.S.

These cases have not only harmed the U.S.-ROC relations, but have also severely undermined the credibility of the KMT government. The Henry Liu murder reinforces the suspicion that the KMT security agencies have all along resorted to such brutal and unlawful acts against dissidents. To this day, the mysterious death of Taiwanese-American professor Wen-cheng Chen of Carnegie-Mellon University after a lengthy interrogation by the TGGH in July 1981, and the murder of the mother and twin daughters of Lin Yi-hsiung, a Taiwanese Provincial Assemblyman, on February 28, 1980, remain unsolved.[2]

Domestically, Taiwan was also hit by its worst financial scandal in the first quarter of 1985. The Cathay affair began with bank runs in February at Taipei Tenth Credit Cooperative, Taiwan's largest savings and loan institution, and the Cathay Investment and Trust Company, another quasi-bank, both controlled by Tsai Chen-chou, a KMT member of the Legislative Yuan. Thousands of creditors lost their savings, with losses totalling several hundred million dollars.

Aside from financial irregularities, the scandal has also exposed serious weaknesses in Taiwan's financial system and official corruption at high levels of the KMT government. Not only did government officials tolerate $197 million in illegal loans to sister companies within the Cathay group, but they also lent over a period of four years more than $2.2 billion to the Cooperative despite its financial difficulties, including $700 million less than a week prior to its demise.

The scandal has led so far to the resignation of two ranking government officials. In March, Economic Minister Hsu Lih-teh, who was Minister of Finance until June 1984 and was often mentioned as a possible future

Premier, stepped down on "moral" grounds. After stalling for almost half a year and under the threat of impeachment, Finance Minister Loh Jen-kang quit. In August two other senior Finance Ministry officials also resigned, three senior government auditors were dismissed for providing Tenth Credit Cooperative with advance warning of official financial examinations, and a dozen other officials were reprimanded.

Also implicated in the scandal was Premier Yu Kuo-hua, who, until becoming Premier in June 1984, was President of the Central Bank and had the final say on financial policy for more than a decade. There is a widespread belief that Yu is ultimately responsible because Ministers Hsu and Loh are known to be his proteges, and an investigative report produced by the Control Yuan, the highest watch-dog body in Taiwan, linked Yu with a decision two years ago not to discipline Tenth Credit Cooperative's management, even though irregularities had been reported to him. Calls for Yu's resignation notwithstanding, Yu remains in office, as he is personally and politically close to President Chiang Ching-kuo. Consequently, the crisis of confidence in the KMT leadership has deepened.

Chiang's Succession

Shortly before the financial crisis at Tenth Credit Cooperative burst open in February, KMT Secretary-General Tsiang Yen-si, who was widely expected to play a major political role after President Chiang, was abruptly removed. The immediate cause of Tsiang's dismissal seemed to have been his rumored involvement in the Cathay scandal. Tsiang was succeeded as the Secretary-General of KMT by the 76-year-old Mah Soo-lay, who was Taiwan's unofficial ambassador in Japan.

The selection of Mah, a caretaker at best, immediately fueled the speculation that Chiang had removed powerful contenders for his mantle from the picture in order to prepare his son, 43-year-old Chiang Hsiao-wu, for succession. Inasmuch as Mah and Chiang Hsiao-wu know each other well and both are officials of the Broadcasting Corporation of China, Mah's appointment was seen by some as part of an effort to advance Hsiao-wu. In order to squelch such speculation once and for all, President Chiang publicly and emphatically stated that the succession would not be a family affair.

Thus, in a speech to the National Assembly on December 25 marking the Constitution Day, President Chiang declared that:

> This sort of question [succession to the Presidency] only exists in despotic and totalitarian countries. It does not exist in the Republic of China, based on the Constitution. So the next President will be elected in accordance with constitutional procedure by the National Assembly on behalf of the

> people. Some people may raise the question whether any member of my family would run for the next Presidency. My answer is: it can't be and it won't be.
>
> The second question: Is there any possibility that our country would be governed by the military? My answer is: it can't be and it won't be. The ruling party has always steered a course based on democracy, liberty, and equality.[3]

As a matter of fact, there has been widespread concern about Chiang's succession in Taiwan, as he is over 75, a diabetic, and has had to undergo surgery three times since 1981. When Chiang was hospitalized in early 1982, an *ad-hoc* group inside the KMT high command, including ex-President Yen Chia-kan; then KMT Secretary-General Tsiang Yen-si; then Premier Sun Yun-suan; General Wang Sheng, then Director of General Political Warfare Department; Shen Chang-huan, then Secretary-General of the National Security Council; and Admiral Ma Chi-chuang, then Secretary-General of the Presidential Office, was set up to prepare for the contingency and a possible transfer of power.[4]

The group was dissolved several months later, after Chiang's health was sufficiently improved, but his succession has remained the most popular topic of private conversations among Taiwan's citizens. After all, Chiang has become the linchpin of Taiwan's polity and precariously held the pieces together—thus acute concern about his succession and the island's future is understandable. In the past several years, many articles have openly but cautiously discussed this sensitive subject. In 1982, when one journal, *Tsong Heng,* devoted 12 pages to evaluating the probable Chiang successors, and another, *Kuo Shih Pinglun,* solicited public opinion on who should succeed Chiang and was going to publish the result of its canvass, they were banned for having crossed the limits of acceptable political discussion.

No doubt, the abrupt ouster of General Wang Sheng in 1983 was closely related to the politics of succession that has simmered in the background in recent years. Wang, who was Director of the General Political Warfare Department (GPWD) and a lifelong associate of President Chiang, was one of the most powerful men in the KMT power structure since the late 1970s and was seen by many as a possible Chiang successor or at least a "king-maker".

A manifestation of such power was the establishment in 1979 of the "Liu Shao-kang Office"—code name of an *ad-hoc* super-policy group consisting of top government, Party, and military leaders like Premier Sun, KMT Secretary-General Tsiang, and Chief of Staff Admiral Sung—with General Wang Sheng as its coordinator. Through this organ Wang had a strong voice in party affairs, government issues, and even foreign policy matters that otherwise would be none of his business. Precisely because Wang had become so powerful, he unavoidably threatened and offended other officials.

The event that contributed to and precipitated Wang's downfall was his semi-official visit to the U.S. in April 1983. Some U.S. officials, in view of Wang's political prominence and no doubt with an eye on his future political role in Taiwan, sought to cultivate him. But the invitation turned out to be a political "kiss of death," since President Chiang Ching-kuo apparently considered the American gesture an attempt to influence the politics of succession and to interfere with the internal affairs of the ROC. His response was swift and decisive. In early May, soon after Wang returned from his unpublicized U.S. trip, Chiang ordered the "Liu Shao-kang Office" disbanded; four days later, on May 9, Chiang transferred Wang from Director of the GPWD to an obscure post as Director of the Department of Joint Operations and Training. In mid-November 1985, Chiang appointed Wang as the ROC Ambassador to Paraguay, thus totally removing him from Taiwan's political scene.[5]

Before President Chiang's first term expired in 1984, several commentators in Taiwan had urged him to stay on as Chairman of the KMT, but to give the Presidency of the ROC to one of his trusted lieutenants. Premier Sun, a technocrat by training and a political moderate, was frequently mentioned as Chiang's most likely successor. In February 1984, the KMT held a Central Committee session and once again nominated Chiang as its Presidential candidate. To the surprise of virtually everyone, however, Chiang named a native of Taiwan, Dr. Lee Teng-hui, who was Governor of Taiwan and a graduate of Cornell University, as his Vice-President. If Sun remained Premier, he could still be a contender for Chiang's mantle as the KMT Chairman upon Chiang's passing, but Sun suffered a severe stroke soon thereafter and had to be replaced, thereby cutting short his political career prematurely.

If President Chiang Kai-Shek's succession in 1975 is any guide, the forthcoming leadership change seems likely to operate at constitutional and informal levels. When the elder Chiang died in April 1975, the Presidency was filled by Vice-President Yen Chia-kan. However, it was Chiang Ching-kuo, the Premier of the Executive Yuan, who succeeeded his father as the KMT Chairman and wielded the real power in that capacity. In 1978, Yen stepped down as President when the term expired, and Ching-kuo was elected to the Presidency.

Likewise, if Ching-kuo dies in office prior to 1990, Vice-President Lee automatically succeeds as President. Whereas some mainlander leaders may not want to see a Taiwan native taking over the presidency, they would be unable constitutionally to deny him the office. Any attempt to contravene established procedures is certain to anger Washington and could cost American support. Moreover, people and officials in the regime realize that Taiwan needs political unity and stability at a time of diplomatic isolation and leadership transition at home, hence they will close ranks behind the constitutional heir.

It should be pointed out emphatically that no future government or party leader after Chiang Ching-kuo is likely to control all the major bases of power and will not possess the undisputed power that Chiang has thus far wielded. The era of one-man rule in Taiwan will come to an end with Chiang's passing, and the post-Chiang Taiwan will witness a collegial rule. Included in the collective leadership will be Lee Teng-hui and other leaders like ex-President Yen Chia-kan, Premier Yu Kuo-hua, Minister of Education Lee Huan, KMT Secretary-General Mah Soo-lay, Chief of Staff General Hau Pei-tsun and Vice-Premier Lin Yang-kang. Together they represent key systems of power—the government, the party, and the military-security apparatus—in the polity.

Taiwan's External Relations

In the wake of the Sino-British agreement on Hong Kong in October 1984, which has provided for the return of Hong Kong to China in 1997, Peking has renewed its appeal to Taiwan to reunify with the motherland. As a matter of fact, ever since the U.S. de-recognition of the ROC government in Taipei in 1979, Peking has launched a series of peace offensives to pressure the KMT government into peace talks. A concrete reunification proposal was made by Peking in 1981, offering to let Taiwan keep its armed forces, autonomy, and existing socio-economic system. In a speech in New York on January 16, 1984, PRC Premier Zhao Ziyang reiterated the proposal:

> After the country is reunified, Taiwan, as a special administrative region of China, can retain much of its own character and keep its social system and life style unchanged. The existing party, government and military setups in Taiwan can also remain unchanged. The central Government will send no representatives or troops to be stationed in Taiwan.
>
> Using the name of "Taiwan: China," Taiwan may also continue its external economic and cultural exchanges, and foreign investments in Taiwan will be fully protected. Of course, the People's Republic of China alone is to represent China in the international arena. In a word, neither party will swallow up the other."[6]

Thus far, Taipei has repeatedly spurned Peking's offer. The reasons behind the KMT's seemingly obdurate stance are many and complex—some pertaining to the obsession and fear of the conservative Chinese

Nationalist leaders, and others pertaining to Taiwanese people's apprehension and opposition.

Three major political considerations appear to have dictated Taipei's hard line and precluded a more flexible response to the communist peace offensive. First of all, inasmuch as the Nationalist government still claims to be the sole legitimate government of China, of which Taiwan is only a province, and justifies on such a claim its authoritarian rule over the native Taiwanese, who comprise 85% of the population on the island, it cannot afford to negotiate with the "Communist bandits" on unification. To accept Peking's proposal for negotiation, not to mention Peking's terms of reunification (which would reduce the KMT government in Taipei to the status of a local government) would, by the KMT's own standards, be tantamount to affirming the legitimacy of the Peking regime as China's rightful government, and at the same time destroy its own main claim to power in Taiwan.

Secondly, at least some KMT officials are fearful that once Taipei consents to conduct the talks for unification, Washington might suspend arms sales to Taipei, either voluntarily or as a result of pressure from the PRC. Such a development would demoralize Taiwan and severely weaken Taipei's position.

Thirdly, many people in Taiwan are strongly anti-Communist and harbor grave apprehensions toward the Peking regime. Hence the KMT leadership does not want unwittingly to alarm the public, or worse, risk a popular uprising, if people on the island—native Taiwanese and mainlanders alike—misconstrue any slight display of interest in negotiations with Peking on the KMT's part as a prelude to "sellout." Thus, the KMT authorities have time and again pledged "no negotiation, no compromise, no contacts" with the Communists.

Many old mainlanders in Taiwan are known to have visited the mainland secretly in recent years, because they want to see their relatives; but they return to Taiwan and do not want to live under Communist rule. Most of the children of mainlanders are quite accustomed to life in Taiwan and share little of their parents' nostalgia or sentimental ties to the mainland. Moreover, not a few Taiwanese businessmen have benefited a great deal from trade with the mainland in recent years. They would be pleased if the ROC authorities would remove restrictions on direct economic exchanges between both sides of the Taiwan strait. It should be stressed, however, that these businessmen want to trade with the mainland, but do not want reunification or to live under a Communist government. Likewise, most Taiwanese feel if Taiwan and the mainland are reunited under the prevailing conditions, they will have little to gain and much more to lose.

Because Peking's peaceful unification campaign has failed to produce the desired response from Taiwan, the Chinese leadership in Peking may have become impatient, and have occasionally threatened the use of force. In October 1984, for instance, China's strongman Deng Xiaoping told Japanese visitors that the PRC would not renounce use of force in "taking back" Taiwan, and that the Chinese military had the capability to blockade the island. In May 1985, Party General Secretary Hu Yaobang went a step further and advocated the use of force to accomplish reunification. In an interview on May 10, 1985, Hu told Lu Keng, publisher of a Chinese newspaper in New York, that ". . . if we are economically powerful in 7, 8, or 10 years, we shall be in a position to modernize our national defense. If the broad masses of the Taiwan people wish to return and a small number of people do not wish to return, it will be necessary to use some force."[7] Hu added: "If we have the strength to enforce a blockade and if Taiwan vehemently opposes reunification, we shall have to consider enforcing a blockade."

In spite of Peking's sabre-rattling, indirect trade and the smuggling of goods between Taiwan and China have increased enormously over the years. According to *Far Eastern Economic Review*, the total indirect trade between Taiwan and China in 1984 amounted to $560 million (with $430 million representing Taiwan's exports to China), and it may exceed $1 billion in 1985. Alarmed by Taiwan's increasing volume of trade with the mainland and apprehensive of Peking's possible sabotage or political blackmail, the KMT authorities prosecuted a number of Taiwanese businessmen who were trading directly with the PRC and fishermen who were engaged in smuggling, obviously intending to intimidate others from direct contacts with the mainland.

Meanwhile, Peking scored some diplomatic gains at Taipei's expense. In July and November 1985, Bolivia and Nicaragua respectively established diplomatic relations with the PRC and severed official ties with the ROC. The number of nations which recognize the ROC is now 23 worldwide. During the year, Vice-President Lee Teng-hui made two trips to Latin America to help shore up Taiwan's diplomatic front, but Peking's stepped-up offensive in the region, including Premier Zhao Ziyang's well-publicized tour of Central and South America in October, began to make inroads.

Likewise, the ROC's status in the Asian Development Bank (ADB) came under a new challenge as Peking formally applied for membership and attached a condition on its entry that the ROC change its name in the ADB to "Taiwan, China." Subsequently, the ADB did admit the PRC as a new member and told the ROC to change its name to "China, Taipei." As part of its strategy to isolate Taiwan in the diplomatic and international arenas, Peking initially sought Taipei's expulsion from the ADB, but when that failed, it adopted the new ploy that was likely to humiliate the KMT authorities and induce Taipei to withdraw voluntarily from the ADB.

Indeed, some hardliners in the KMT leadership wanted to walk out of the ADB—the most important international body and one of the very few intergovernmental organizations to which the ROC still belongs. They contended that to remain in the ADB under the new name would make the ROC look like a provincial unit of the PRC and undermine the raison d'être of KMT rule in Taiwan. Thus, Foreign Minister Chu Fu-sung stated on several occasions that the ROC would not ". . . accept any arrangement which contradicts the ADB charter or affects this nation's status, interest, or name."

An alarmed Reagan administration dispatched William Clark, President Reagan's former National Security Advisor, to Taipei in November to dissuade the ROC government from such a diplomatically suicidal course. At the behest of the U.S. government, Prime Minister Lee Kuan Yew of Singapore, a close personal friend of President Chiang, also visited Taipei in November to help persuade the ROC government to adopt a more flexible approach toward the ADB.[8]

At home, scores of KMT and non-KMT members of the Legislative Yuan (congress), in an unprecedented move, submitted a joint statement questioning the government's policy. Many scholars and opinion-makers also spoke out in favor of staying in the ADB under the new name. Some even sharply criticized the "all or nothing" approach advocated by a number of ultra-conservative officials.

After considerable internal debate, the KMT government settled on a compromise decision and declared that it would not accept the change of name, would not withdraw from the ADB, and would not attend the ADB meetings to protest the arrangement imposed by the ADB. The "3-no" position is highly unpopular in Taiwan and has been widely criticized for being unrealistic, quixotic and flouting public opinion.

Economic Slowdown and Open Door

Taiwan's economy experienced a severe downturn in 1985. Its economic growth plunged from a 10.5 percent rate in 1984 to 4.73 percent in 1985, far below the initially projected 8.5 percent. The sharp decline was due partly to a slowdown in exports to the U.S., which has taken close to 50 percent of Taiwan's exports in recent years. Taiwan's exports grew only 1 percent in the first half of 1985, compared with 12 percent in the same period in 1984.

Another cause of Taiwan's economic decline can be attributed to the Cathay financial scandal, which prompted the government to tighten credit by banks and underground money lenders, and thus reduce further domestic investment. In fact, gross fixed-capital formation has been at a standstill since 1981. Taken as a proportion of gross national product, investment declined from nearly 30 percent in the early 1980s to 23 percent in 1984 and below 20 percent through the first half of 1985.[9]

To reserve such a trend, which threatens to slow economic growth for years to come, and to cope with other economic, financial, and trade problems facing Taiwan's economy, the government set up a special cabinet-level task force in April, called the Economic Revitalization Committee (ERC), composed of government officials, industrial representatives, and scholars, to come up with solutions. After 21 full sessions, 69 panel meetings, and 110 workshop discussions, the ERC has made 56 recommendations, ranging from reforms in taxation to economic administration.

There is a consensus among the knowledgeable observers that the government must undertake extensive reforms of an archaic economic and financial structure, do away with cumbersome, rigid government regulations and excessive control, and lighten the heavy tax burden, among other things. Publicly the government has thanked the ERC for a job well done and stated that it would carefully study the recommendations. In private, some top government officials are known to feel that most of the proposed changes are too drastic to be implemented.

On the other hand, responding to heavy American government pressure to correct the trade imbalance, which amounted to 9.8 billion in 1984 and at least $10 billion in 1985 in Taiwan's favor, and mindful of the Jenkins Bill, which, if passed, could cost an estimated $1 billion in Taiwan's exports of textiles and garments to the U.S. and 70,000 jobs in Taiwan, Taipei removed some of its own protectionist measures and lowered import barriers. American beers, wines and cigarettes will be sold in the Taiwan market in 1986. The Customs Administration cut an import surcharge levied on all products to 5 percent from the 20 percent set two years earlier, and said it would be removed in 1986.

In recent years, Taiwan has taken action against commercial pirates. Already it has passed a new trademark law with penalties of up to five years' imprisonment for violators, and allowed foreign corporations that registered their trademarks and patents in Taiwan to file criminal suits in courts to fight trademark and patent infringements. In June 1985, the Legislative Yuan passed a bill which substantially stiffened penalties against copyright infringement and explicitly protected computer software.

Calling for Policy and Leadership Changes

On November 16, 1985, local elections were held in Taiwan to choose 77 provincial assemblymen, city council members for Taipei (52) and Kaohsiung (41), and 21 county chiefs and mayors. These elections, held every three years, drew 357 candidates who vied for 191 seats, and slightly more than 70 percent of the eligible voters cast their votes.

The election campaign, which lasted for ten days, was quite lively. One of the campaign's most striking features was that it served as a public forum for the non-KMT candidates to attack government policies and to advocate fundamental political changes. Furthermore, the election campaign became a "holiday for freedom of expression" as opposition candidates openly aired such politically sensitive issues as self-determination on Taiwan's destiny by its 19 million people. To the credit of the government, which has been at pains to demonstrate progress toward democratization and greater political freedom so as to prove the KMT regime worthy of continued U.S. support, no actions were taken to stop public discussion of these political taboos.

In spite of the KMT government's longstanding ban on the establishment of rival political parties, the *Tangwai*, Taiwan's loose opposition grouping, set up an *ad-hoc* Candidates' Aid Committee to nominate its candidate and help their campaign activities. Notwithstanding political and personal differences which have plagued the opposition camp for years, the Committee did produce a slate of 42 candidates. They were to face a slate of 157 KMT candidates, who were younger and better educated than ever before, 88 percent of whom were native Taiwanese.

In the elections, the KMT won 38 of the 52 seats in Taipei City Council, but all 11 candidates who were nominated by the Tangwai Candidates' Aid Committee were also elected. In fact, out of the 42 candidates nominated and endorsed by the Committee, 34 won, sending political shockwaves throughout the KMT headquarters. Overall, the Tangwai and other non-KMT candidates won more popular votes, approximately 33 percent, and a few more seats, than in previous elections, and could claim a moral victory.

On the other hand, the KMT retained 146 of the 191 contested posts, including 17 of 21 contested county chiefs and mayoralties (one more seat than in the last election). However, the elections were marred by reports of vote-buying, irregularities, and fraud in several localities, and demonstrators in Hsin-Chu hurled stones at government offices and overturned cars in protest against alleged ballot rigging by the ruling party. In light of the scandals and setbacks suffered by the government during the year, the election results were quite gratifying to the ruling party, and the government spokesmen were quick to claim the electoral victory as a vote of confidence by the people.

To the detached observer, such self-complacency and arrogance is out of line with Taiwan's political reality. Among Taiwan's concerned citizens, there is widespread discontent over the scandals, diplomatic setbacks, inability of the government to cope with the economic slump, violent crimes, and the poor quality of government leadership. There is a crisis of confidence, despite denials by government spokesmen. President Chiang Ching-kuo seems aware of such popular sentiment, and he alluded to it in his speech to the National Assembly on December 25: "Although I have been trying my best in my position, there have been several misfortunes that brought about distress to our country and our people during this period, some of them caused by nature, others the result of human error, and I have been deeply disturbed."

In the same speech, President Chiang also states that he would ". . . continue to work hard with perseverance and determination to overcome all adversities and to bring about a bright future for our country in the days to come." But how? When the KMT announced in early December that it would convene a Central Committee Plenum in March 1986, there was a chorus of reactions from various social circles urging reshuffles in the KMT Central Executive Committee and the Executive Yuan (cabinet) to bring fresh blood into these bodies and calling for changes in internal and external policy.[10] The pressure is building for President Chiang to act. The question remains whether he is able and willing to exert the kind of leadership vigor, imagination, and dynamism which he displayed in the 1970s.

Notes

1. Following standard practice in Taiwan, Chinese words in this chapter are given in Wade-Giles romanization rather than in *pinyin*. In cases where individuals prefer a non-standard romanization for their own names, that preference is followed.

2. Mr. Lin was sentenced to a 16-year jail term on charges of sedition after he took part in a Human Rights Day rally in Kaohsiung on December 9, 1979, which degenerated into a massive riot. In July 1984, the ROC commuted Lin's sentence and permitted him to leave Taiwan and come to Los Angeles, where he is now living with his daughter, who survived the terrorist assassination in February 1980, and his wife, who won a seat in the Legislative Yuan during the 1983 parliamentary elections.

3. *The Free China Journal* (Taipei), December 30, 1985, p.1.

4. None of those in the inner circles of the KMT power structure was a native Taiwanese.

5. Admiral Ma Chi-Chuan, who was formerly the Secretary-General of the Presidential Office, and had the audacity to assert power and make major decisions when the President was ill, has met the same fate. In June 1984, he was transferred out of the Presidential Office and appointed Minister of State without portfolio, and in December 1985 named Taipei's new representative to Japan to head the Association of East Asian Relations in Tokyo.

6. *The New York Times*, January 17, 1984.

7. "Hu Yaobang Interviewed by Pai Hsing's Lu Keng," *Foreign Broadcast Information Service, Daily Report, China*, June 3, 1985, W7.

8. Prime Minister Lee has visited Taiwan many times in the past without publicity, but this trip was announced to the public in advance.

9. *Asia 1986 Yearbook* (Hong Kong: Far Eastern Economic Review), p. 246.

10. See, for example, *Independent Evening News* (Taipei), December 5, 1985.

1985: A Chronology

JANUARY

Deng Xiaoping's book, *Build Socialism with Chinese Characteristics,* in which he asserts that the open door policy will not lead China to capitalism, is published.

Accords on economic, technical and scientific cooperation are signed by Soviet First Deputy Premier Ivan Arkhipov in Beijing.

President Li Xiannian meets with Cambodian President Sihanouk in Beijing.

State announced 169 key projects for 1985, 60 of which concern energy development.

General John Vessey, Chairman of the United States Joint Chiefs of Staff, arrives in Beijing on official visit.

Dutch Foreign Minister Hans van den Broek arrives in Beijing on official visit.

9th meeting of the National Party Congress Standing Committee opens with Peng Zhen presiding.

Student protest at Beijing University over elimination of educational stipends ends in compromise by the University.

State Councilor, Chen Muhua leaves on official trade mission to Europe.

Mother Teresa arrives in Beijing as guest of Chinese Patriotic Catholic Association.

President Li and Premier Zhao send congratulatory message to President Reagan on his reelection.

U.N. group pledges aid to PRC family planning in wake of protests about Chinese birth control practices.

FEBRUARY

Chinese Communist Party Central Discipline Inspection Commission urges party leadership to act against officials who are profiteering or squandering public funds.

Chinese Communist Youth League Central Committee sets up national association for factory and business administrators 35 years old or younger calling them "the mainstay of China's current economic reform."

A "responsible person" of the CPC Central Committee in Xinhua interview affirms the need to promote the new generation in order to achieve victories for the modernization program and for reforms.

23rd Session of U.N. Population Commission addressed by Chinese delegation leader, Wu Jieping, who stresses the need for understanding of the global, long-term significance of the population problem.

Foreign Minister Wu Xueqian meets in Beijing with the U.S. Assistant Secretary of State, Paul Wolfowitz to discuss international bilateral issues of common concern.

World Bank loans China $117 million for electrical development.

Chinese government announces that prices for agricultural and industrial commodities will now fluctuate according to market demands; state procurement quotas for agricultural products abolished.

MARCH

PRC parliamentary delegation leaves on official visit to USSR.

President Li Xiannian leaves on visit to Burma and Thailand.

PRC leaders offer condolences on death of Soviet leader Constantin Chernenko; Vice Premier Li Peng leads delegation to funeral.

8th meeting of CPPCC 6th National Committee convenes, electing 40 new members to the National Committee.

Central Committee issues science and technology reform decision aimed at integrating science and technology with economic construction.

U.S. Undersecretary of State Michael Armacost visits Beijing to hold foreign-policy talks.

Premier Zhao Ziyang calls for increased exchange with the United States.

APRIL

Document on PRC-USSR trade, transportation in 1985 signed during visit of Chinese delegation to Moscow.

Premier Zhao, Foreign Minister Wu meet with Arab League Delegation in Beijing.

PRC announced Hong Kong will be allowed to keep existing religious institutions after 1997.

Queen Elizabeth II signs UK-HK bill ending term of British rule July 1, 1997.

Foreign Minister Wu Xueqian leaves on visit to Philippines.

300 youths, sent down to the countryside during the Cultural Revolution, protest in Beijing and are ordered to return to Shanxi.

Han Xu appointed new Ambassador to the United States.

Party Secretary Hu Yaobang leaves on visit to Australia, New Zealand and Papua New Guinea.

MAY

Yasir Arafat leads Jordan-PLO delegation to PRC.

PRC announces it will levy industrial and commercial consolidated tax and enterprise income tax on China-based offices of foreign, Hong Kong, and Macao companies.

PRC soccer loss to Hong Kong results in Beijing violence against foreigners.

China to begin military training in selected high schools and colleges as a first step in implementing new, compulsory, military service law adopted at 1984 National People's Congress.

Chinese newspaper providing information on transfer of military technology to civilian circles begins publication.

CPC announces educational reform policy stressing division of skills, technical education, compulsory 9-year middle school education, and more autonomy for colleges with the initiation of summer school and dual majors at Beijing University.

U.S. postpones first visit since 1949 of warships to Shanghai after controversy over whether ships were nuclear-armed and powered.

Hong Kong lawyer Hanson Huang Xian, imprisoned in China for espionage, paroled by Beijing Intermediate People's Court.

JUNE

Premier Zhao Ziyang, Foreign Minister Wu Xueqian head delegation visiting UK.

PRC declares restructuring of communes complete with 56,000 communes now replaced by 92,000 small towns and township governments.

Chinese government announces it will reduce numbers in PLA by one million within the next two years. Many older officers are to retire; younger, professionally-trained officers to be promoted. The Defense Ministry announced that General Li Desheng, China's longest-serving military chief, would be retired under this new policy.

PRC soccer team disbanded with coach resigning in wake of May riots.

National People's Congress began its 11th session. Eight new ministers appointed (average age 54.6) to accelerate the process of replacement of old by new.

JULY

First full session of Hong Kong basic law drafting committee ends in Beijing with Chinese leaders calling it a successful first step in drafting the territory's future constitution.

Party marks 64th anniversary of CPC founding with celebrations.

Vice-Premier Li Peng meets with U.S. House Committee delegation in Beijing.

Deng Ligun relieved of post as head of Party Propaganda department after his spiritual pollution campaign; Zhu Houze replaces him.

President Li Xiannian begins U.S. visit; meets with President Reagan; two presidents sign accord on peaceful uses of nuclear technology.

China announces $6.41 billion January-June trade deficit.

Turkish Prime Minister Turgut Ozal visits Beijing, meeting with Deng Xiaoping who tells him China's current pragmatic economic reforms are an experiment.

Vice Premier Yao Yilin visits Moscow and signs two new long-term economic and trade agreements with the Soviet Union.

China announces foreign investment is to be channeled into Shanghai, Canton, Dalian and Tianjin with de-emphasis on other 10 coastal cities opened to outside trade in 1984.

Suharto of Indonesia authorizes direct trade between China and Indonesia.

AUGUST	UNESCO meeting on exchange of scientific information held in Beijing.
	American sentenced to 18 months in PRC jail for his part in hotel fire.
	Japanese Prime Minister Nakasone's visit to Yasukuni shrine draws criticism from Japanese and other Asian groups.
	China sends representatives to Hiroshima Anti-nuclear meeting; Premier Zhao Ziyang sends telegram to Japanese A-bomb victims.
	Renmin Ribao editorial praises Li's visit to U.S., stressing Reagan's participation despite recent operation as evidence of store he sets by U.S.-China relations.
	Indonesian trade delegation visits China to re-establish official trade links, talks with Chinese officials.
SEPTEMBER	10,000 attend assembly held in Beijing to mark 40th anniversary of War of Resistance against Japan. Party calls for third round of cooperation between KMT and CCP; one country, two systems.
	PRC government announces all Chinese citizens 16 years and over must apply for resident's ID cards.

Ten people out of the 24-member politburo and 18% of the 210-member central committee hand in resignations because of "declining energy" to facilitate socialist modernization. Lifelong tenure for leading posts to be eliminated. Party declares that with this step the readjustment of principal administrative organs is considered basically completed.

1,000 Beijing University students stage an anti-Japanese demonstration, commemorating the September 18 incident, in reaction to the Japanese Prime Minister's visit to Yasukuni shrine.

Foreign Minister Wu Xueqian leaves for New York to attend the U.N. Session.

United States withholds U.N. Fund for Population Activities monies after protests on Chinese birth control policies.

China replaces chiefs of police and state security in reorganization which brought younger men to head five ministries.

Deng Xiaoping meets with Singapore Prime Minister Lee Kuan Yew in Beijing.

Soviet Foreign Minister, Eduard Shevardnadze holds talks with Wu Xueqian at U.N. in New York. Both parties agree to exchange visits.

OCTOBER

U.S. Senate approves Winston Lord as envoy to PRC.

Party announces drive to recruit new members from "advanced" elements, such as model workers. Says more than 1.4 million entered party last year.

Vice-President Bush arrives in Beijing for visit; meets with Premier Zhao, Vice-Premier Wan Li and Party Secretary Hu Yaobang.

Premier Zhao leaves on official visit to U.S. to attend 40th Anniversary of U.N. founding.

About 9,000 cadre-run businesses shut down due to officials' illegal use of their connections for profit-making purposes.

Boom in martial arts books causes paper shortage threatening textbook publication.

Xian students stage anti-Japanese demonstration.

Delegates from Supreme Soviet, headed by Chairman Lev Tolkunov, visit China to resume discussions on how to normalize their strained relations after a 20-year break.

Rumanian President, Nicolae Ceausescu arrives in Beijing on official visit.

West German Foreign Minister Hans-Dietrick Genscher arrives in Beijing for official visit.

Chinese delegation visits North Korea to mark 35th Anniversary of entry of Chinese forces into Korean War.

NOVEMBER

Former Secretary of State Henry Kissinger begins "private" visit to PRC, meets with Deng Xiaoping, Li Xiannian and Hu Yaobang.

Provincial financial inspections in PRC reveal misconduct in excess of $3.51 billion yuan.

China News Agency reports that beginning March, 1986, China Travel Service-organized trips to Hong Kong and Macao to meet relatives will be expanded to all provinces and municipalities except Tibet.

Bishop Fu of the Beijing Diocese leads the first delegation of PRC Catholics to Belgium. Catholics from all over Western Europe travel to Belgium to make contact.

Court releases American jailed in hotel fire on probation.

Malaysian Prime Minister Datuk Seri Mahathir Mohamad and a 130-member delegation arrive in Beijing on official visit to discuss trade and other economic relations.

Hundreds of students, watched closely by police, gather in Tiananmen Square in a silent protest apparently directed against Japan.

Politburo member Hu Qili meets with West German Chancellor Helmut Kohl in Bonn.

U.S. Assistant Secretary of State Paul Wolfowitz arrives in Beijing to brief Chinese leaders on the Geneva summit.

DECEMBER

Former Vice-President Walter Mondale visits PRC meeting with Deng Xiaoping.

U.S. House of Representatives passes Textile Import Quota Bill which is then vetoed by President Reagan.

"Defense University," a high-level military academy to train military commanders is founded in Beijing.

Beijing University minority students from Xinjiang rally to protest nuclear testing in their province, coercive family-planning among minorities, and to demand increased representation of minorities in provincial government and increased support for minority education.

Soviet Deputy Foreign Minister and Senior China Specialist, M.S. Kapitsa visits China.

Vice-Premier Li Peng visits Bulgaria and Czechoslovakia.

President Reagan signs Congressional resolution on nuclear pact with PRC, first negotiated during his 1984 visit to China, after restrictions added to agreement, opposed by both U.S. and Chinese governments, were dropped.

U.S. Commerce Secretary Malcolm Baldridge announces the U.S. will ease restrictions on the export of computers, machine tools, semi-conductors, electronic instruments, raising the categories of products that can be exported to China without special review from 7 to 27.

Rumanian foreign trade minister visits Beijing meeting with Vice-Premier Wan Li and signing trade protocol.

Premier Zhao Ziyang visits Colombia, Brazil, Argentina, Venezuela in first time ever visit of Chinese Premier to Latin America.

NOTE: This chronology is based on "The Week" section of *Far Eastern Economic Review, Foreign Broadcast Information Service (Daily Report, China),* and *Beijing Review.*

About the Contributors

David Bachman is assistant professor of politics at Princeton University.

Parris H. Chang is professor of political science at Pennsylvania State University. During 1985-86 he was visiting professor at the Department of Strategic and Area Studies, JFK Special Warfare Center, Fort Bragg, N.C.

John S. Major is director of the China Council of The Asia Society.

Barry J. Naughton is assistant professor of economics at the University of Oregon.

Elizabeth J. Perry is an associate professor on the faculty of the Henry M. Jackson School of International Studies at the University of Washington.

Peter J. Seybolt is professor of history at the University of Vermont.

Richard P. Suttmeier is a senior analyst in the International Security and Commerce Program, Office of Technology Assessment, United States Congress.

Michael B. Yahuda is a member of the faculty of the International Relations Department, London School of Economics. During 1985-86, he was a visiting professor at the Center for Chinese Studies, University of Michigan.

Index